Christ
Crucified

Christ Crucified

The once-for-all sacrifice

STEPHEN CHARNOCK

INTRODUCTION BY J. I. PACKER

CHRISTIAN
HERITAGE

Introduction © J. I Packer 1996

© Christian Focus Publications, Ltd.

ISBN 978-1-84550-976-7

Published in 1996, reprinted in 2002 and 2012
by
Christian Focus Publications
Geanies House, Fearn,
Ross-shire, IV20 1TW, Scotland, United Kingdom

Cover design
by
Paul Lewis

Printed by
Bell and Bain, Glasgow

CONTENTS

INTRODUCTION

The central fact in Christianity is the reality, historical, eternal and inescapable, of Jesus Christ, who is the Son of God in the trinitarian sense of being God the Son, who is the future Judge of all human beings everywhere, and whom the gospel proclaims as Saviour, Redeemer and Friend to all who become His followers. Let us be clear that where Jesus is not acknowledged as God incarnate, crucified, risen, reigning and returning, there is no Christianity, whatever liberals in and outside the churches may say to the contrary.

Again, the central focus in Christianity is the knowledge, conceptual and relational, objective and personal, of Christ crucified. This is a knowledge that involves both the head and the heart, and that begets a new loyalty, a new love and a new life. It is the theme with which the Puritan Stephen Charnock is dealing in the work that I am here introducing. Let us be clear that apart from this knowledge there are no Christians, and it is mere confusion not to recognise this.

Charnock, ministering in nominally Christian Britain three centuries ago, could count on general assent to the positions I have just stated. But that is something no Christian communicator today dare do. The man in the street, as we like to say (and the woman in the street, as feminists would like us to say) sees Christianity as a moral code rather than as good news of salvation, and Jesus as a dead teacher rather than a living Saviour, and spiritual life as New Age-type meditation for self-improvement, and religious commitment as a hobby for those who care about that sort of thing. That we all live in God's presence and under His eye, and that we must one day answer to him for the lives we have lived, and that our humanity is so out of shape through sin that we need a Saviour as urgently as persons with brain tumours need a surgeon, are truths that never enter most people's minds. In this climate of opinion it is no wonder if Christians themselves become unclear and uncertain about central elements in their own faith. If we do, however, that is all the more reason why we should listen to Charnock, who of all the Puritans is the most brisk and businesslike when it comes to saying things straight.

Charnock assumes that those he addresses are interested in his themes, and so are willing to concentrate on his unfolding of them. In his day many were: 'able ministers' (so his first editors tell us) 'loved to sit at his feet, for they received by one sermon of his those instructions which they could not get by many books or sermons of others'.[1] Popular communication today, however, rarely confronts us with anything so concentrated as a paragraph of Charnock, and unless his readers are seriously concerned they will flag. Perhaps I can do something to generate or reinforce a concern in the hearts of you who read this that will ensure

---

1   *Works of Stephen Charnock* (Edinburgh: James Nichol, 1864), I.xxiv.

that you don't flag when you get to Charnock – let us see. I may fail, I know – but it will not be for want of trying! First, however, a further word about Charnock himself.

Stephen Charnock, 1628–1680

Born in London, and born again at Cambridge University some time in the 1640s, Charnock was seen as a coming man, and was sent to Dublin as chaplain to Oliver Cromwell's son Henry, governor of Ireland, in 1655. There he gained a great reputation as a preacher. The Restoration, however, ended his Irish ministry, and he had no stated charge thereafter till he was called to share with Thomas Watson the pastorate of an elite nonconforming congregation that met in London at Crosby Hall. That lasted five years, from 1675 to his death in 1680. A passionately studious man, apparently a bachelor, he ordinarily put in five twelve-hour days per week in his study, and wrote out everything he proposed to say in public. It seems that he conceived the idea of preaching a complete systematico-practical theology (as we needs must call it) at Crosby Hall, and that his massive unfinished Discourses on the Existence and Attributes of God (over 600,000 words and 1,000 pages of smallish print in the 1864 edition of his collected works) were the start of it. (He died, we are told, while 'looking what to say next of the mercy, grace, and goodness of God'.[2]) These Discourses are giant-size Puritan sermons, each built on a text and laid out with doctrine, reason (exposition and defence), and use (application) in the standard Puritan manner, and each of them, given in full, would have occupied several hour-long preachments. Perhaps Charnock actually delivered them this way; and

---

2   Ibid., I.xxv.

perhaps this, plus the fact that at Crosby Hall his failing memory and eyesight obliged him to read his sermon scripts through a magnifying glass, word for word, instead of speaking extempore without notes as in Dublin, helps to explain why many, even in that theological age, found him both heavy and over their heads, despite the easy handling of ideas that is one of his chief strengths. His smaller-scale treatment of Christ's death, however, flows very simply and will not baffle today's attentive reader in any way.

The Cross of Christ

I said at the outset that where the Lord Jesus is not confessed as God incarnate, crucified, risen, reigning and returning, and where there is no focus on the personal knowledge of Christ crucified, there is no Christianity. When I said that, bold as it sounds, I was defining Christianity in New Testament terms. For in the New Testament the cross of Christ is highlighted as, so to speak, the hinge and fulcrum of the gospel, the event that opened for us sinners a path to peace with God, power from God, and a prospect of glory through God that exceeds our wildest dreams. The gospels, as is often noted, are precisely passion stories with detailed introductions, telling us what led to the crucifixion so that we understand it when it comes. The vivid detail and calculated poignancy with which Matthew, Mark, Luke, and John, four skilful authors, tell the story of the cross exceed in intensity all that precedes, and the resurrection reports that follow, and thus identify the passion of Jesus as the true climax of each gospel. The theme of the book of Revelation is the twofold triumph of the crucified Lord, the slain Lamb, namely that which was at His first coming when He shed His blood for us and that which will be at His second coming when all is made new. And in the epistles, which are sermons about discipleship in letter form, the cross is central and basic to all the formative teaching that is given with regard to both faith (that is to say, belief and trust) and conduct (that is to say, motivation and action).

To be specific. The cross is the burden of the apostolic gospel ('we preach Christ crucified', 1 Cor. 1:23; cf. 1:18; 2:2). It is the centrepiece of God's eternal plan of grace ('you were redeemed ... with the precious blood of Christ, a lamb ... chosen before the creation ... revealed in these last times for your sake,' 1 Pet. 1:18-20; cf. John. 3:16 f.; 10:14-18; Gal. 4:4 f.). It is a sacrifice for sins ('Christ died for our sins according to the Scriptures,' 1 Cor. 15;3), quenching the divine wrath against sinners ('making peace through his blood, shed on the cross', Col. 1:20; cf. Eph. 2:18-20), securing our present justification and adoption and guaranteeing our future hope as God's heirs ('Since we have now been justified by his blood, how much more shall we be saved from God's wrath through him!', Rom. 5:9; 'He who did not spare his own Son, but gave him up for us all – how will he not also, along with him, graciously give us all things?' Rom. 8:32). It is the mediatorial initiative (for Christ's passion was truly His action) that established Him in His saving role, as the author of salvation and so the proper object of saving faith ('The life I live ... I live by faith in the Son of God, who loved me and gave himself for me', Gal. 2:20; 'through faith in his blood', Rom. 3:25). It is the reality signified by the two sacramental ordinances that Jesus imposed ('baptised into his death ... buried with him through baptism into death', Rom. 6:3, 4; 'This is my body, which is for you' ... 'This cup is the new covenant in my blood; do this, whenever you drink it, in remembrance of me', 1 Cor. 11:24-25). It sets us standards of self-giving love and self-denying humility ('live a life of love, just as Christ loved us and gave himself up for us', Eph. 5:2; 'Jesus Christ laid down his life for us. And we ought to lay down our lives for our brothers', 1 John 3:16; 'he humbled himself and became obedient to death - even death on a cross', Phil. 2:8). It calls for, and calls forth, consecrated service and devotion ('You are not your own; you were bought at a price. Therefore honour God with your body', 1 Cor. 6:19, 20; 'Christ's love compels us ... one died for all ... that those who live should no longer live for themselves, but for him who died for them', 2 Cor. 5:14, 15). It models endurance in the face of hostility and pain ('Christ suffered for you, leaving you an example, that you should follow in his steps', 1 Pet. 2:21; cf. Heb. 12:2 f.).

So we might go on, but surely the point is clear enough by now. Trusting, loving and following Jesus necessitates keeping the cross in view at all times. Our living Lord calls for what we may call cruciform discipleship, clear-headed, open-eyed and whole-hearted. 'May I never boast except in the cross of our Lord Jesus Christ, through which the world has been crucified to me, and I to the world' (Gal. 6:14). The cross must shape our faith, and thereby reshape our entire lives.

Celebrating Christ Crucified

Charnock's expositions, though clear and deep, sometimes seem cool and dry. This is because his style is intensely analytical, and his mind moves fast and verbalises itself economically, as if he were writing notes for an exposition rather than composing the exposition itself. His power of boiling down and compressing excites admiration, but can leave the wisdom and truth he sets forth still at a distance from our inner being. As his portrait depicts him as having bony features,[3] so his writing reveals him as a man of bony thoughts who sees it as our part rather than his to put flesh on the bones and warm up the thoughts so that they gain heart-piercing power. The Puritan ideal was to be a 'practical affectionate divine', meaning one who cleared heads, strengthened hearts, and settled consciences with equal skill; Charnock is as strong as any in clearing heads, but is less able than some to stir the imagination and touch the heart. It must have been this distancing of himself as a communicator from the affectional side of life that led some to complain that his sermons had in them only 'morality or metaphysics'[4] – for they contain, not too little evangelical doctrine, but, if anything, too much, packed too tight. Evidently he thought that the dramatising and interiorising of gospel truth was for his hearers to do by personal meditation, rather than for him to attempt by pulpit rhetoric.

Here, he deals with the theme of Christ crucified by dwelling successively on the sovereignty, love and justice of the Father who ordained the cross, the dignity, willingness and agony of the Son in enduring it, the transformed relationship with God that flows from it, and the gratitude, delight, and enlarging of repentance, faith, boldness in approaching God, holiness as a life-goal, and 'comfort' (encouragement) as a life-support, that knowledge of Christ crucified should engender in us. The Reformed and Puritan understanding of penal substitution at Calvary is expressed with plain and simple precision. But it is a cool, bony

3   Ibid., I.xxiv.

4   Ibid., I.xxiii.

treatment, which it is left to us to warm up for ourselves. How shall we do that? I offer the following suggestion. Before you start to read Charnock, spend time with the following three lyrics, each of which embodies some knowledge of Christ crucified in meditations that touch the depths of the Christian heart. Let them search you, and move you, as they are well calculated to do.[5] The first is by the latter-day Puritan, Isaac Watts. It is well known.

When I survey the wondrous cross
On which the Prince of glory died,
My richest gain I count but loss,
And pour contempt on all my pride.

Forbid it, Lord, that I should boast
Save in the death of Christ my God:
All the vain things that charm me most,
I sacrifice them to his blood.

See from his head, his hands, his feet,
Sorrow and love flow mingled down;
Did e'er such love and sorrow meet,
Or thorns compose so rich a crown?

Were the whole realm of nature mine,
That were an offering far too small;
Love so amazing, so divine,
Demands my soul, my life, my all.

The second is also by Isaac Watts. It is less familiar, and more heart-wrenching.

Alas! and did my Saviour bleed
And did my Sovereign die?

---

5   Quoted from Christian Hymns (Bridgend: Evangelical Movement of Wales, second ed., 1985), nos. 203, 197, 540.

Would he devote that sacred head
For such a worm as I?

Was it for crimes that I had done
He groaned upon the tree?
Amazing pity! grace unknown!
And love beyond degree!

Well might the sun in darkness hide,
And shut his glories in,
When God, the mighty Maker, died
For man, the creature's sin.

Thus might I hide my blushing face
While his dear cross appears;
Dissolve my heart in thankfulness,
And melt my eyes to tears.

But drops of grief can ne'er repay
The debt of love I owe:
Here, Lord, I give myself away;
'Tis all that I can do.

The third is by Augustus Toplady, an eighteenth-century evangelical, author of 'Rock of Ages'. It is not at all well known in the modern Christian world. It deals with the self-doubt and inner dread that all regenerate persons face sooner or later.

From whence this fear and unbelief?
Hath not the Father put to grief
His spotless Son for me?
And will the righteous Judge of men
Condemn me for that debt of sin
Which, Lord, was charged on thee?

Complete atonement thou hast made,
And to the utmost thou hast paid
Whate'er thy people owed;

How then can wrath on me take place,
If sheltered in thy righteousness,
And sprinkled with thy blood?

If thou hast my discharge procured
And freely in my room endured
The whole of wrath divine,
Payment God cannot twice demand,
First at my bleeding Surety's hand
And then again at mine.

Turn then, my soul, unto thy rest!
The sorrows of thy great High Priest
Have bought thy liberty;
Trust in his efficacious blood,
Nor fear thy banishment from God,
Since Jesus died for thee.

Now, with the preciousness of the cross to you firmly fixed in your mind and heart through meditating on these lyrics, read Charnock, looking for the full-scale theology that underlies, and justifies, the low thoughts of yourself, and the high thoughts of God the Father and God the Son, with which your broodings have left you. I think you will find that sentence after sentence in Charnock's ordered march lights up and glows in your heart, as illuminating and undergirding things you are feeling. End by working through the lyrics again, elaborating to yourself in God's presence what they say about what has specially struck you in Charnock's presentation. This is only a suggestion, and you are free to ignore it. But please don't accuse Charnock of being dry till you've tried it! That's all I ask.

J.I. Packer

From the Editor

Those who are familiar with Puritan books will not need any word of introduction by a modern writer to recommend them. They will have discovered already that in point of depth, fulness and accuracy the English Puritans excelled when they handled any subject of Christian doctrine or practice and that Puritan books are golden.

It is one of the happiest signs in the religious world today that more and more Christians are 'discovering' the Puritans for themselves. Forty years ago such works were being read by only a small number, often in isolated or remote places such as the Scottish Highlands where the pure gospel still survived unspoilt by the Liberalism of the nineteenth century or the shallow evangelicalism of the early twentieth.

However, the 1950s witnessed a remarkable new development. Beginning in Britain and America at roughly the same time, moves were made by a small number of Christian leaders, who had themselves been drawn to appreciate Puritan theology, to begin the task of reprinting a few choice volumes for the modern reader. It was a venture of faith on the part of such publishers. It might easily have failed and come to nothing. There were not a few critics who pooh-poohed the whole idea of bringing back such old writings and who predicted that it was an enterprise doomed to failure from the start.

But all such gloomy forecasts proved to be wrong and ill-judged. The facts are that interest in these great seventeenth-century divines (as the preachers of that age are respectfully termed) shot up almost overnight. Their books, now dressed up in tasteful modern jackets, were bought up almost as fast as they could be reprinted. Their names became household words in the circles where they were being eagerly read: John Bunyan, Thomas Watson, John Owen, Thomas Goodwin, John Flavel, Richard Baxter, William Gurnall, Stephen Charnock ...

The present writer has not the least doubt that the reprinting of these Puritan volumes, which has gone on steadily from that day to this, occurred through a special gracious act of God's providence. The time was right. The moment for their rediscovery had come. That was the starting point of this modern recovery of the Puritans and their writings, and it occurred in the 1950s.

Today, it would be true to say, there are many publishers who are devoting their energies to this one great task of making the best religious writings of the seventeenth century available to the modern reader. Through the work of editing and abridging, the Puritans are also being brought out in basic, simplified English for readers too busy to handle them in their original size and format. And this, in turn, has meant that, through the good offices of missionaries and devoted Christians in other countries, some Puritan works are available in languages in which they have never appeared till now.

To enthusiasts like the present writer, all this makes very welcome and good news and is a matter for deep thankfulness to God. Largely unnoticed by the secular press and media, a movement of worldwide extent is taking place in our generation by which some of the richest, deepest and finest Puritan teaching is again becoming available to the English-speaking world – and also, for the first time ever in some cases, to people of other languages as well.

What we here report as to the springing up of brand new interest in Puritanism in many parts of the world can only be explained, as we have above explained it, as a gracious act of God's providence and nothing less.

It is well known that our modern world is being everywhere and increasingly bombarded by what is cheap, worthless and impure. Standards have gone down in both journalism and the media. Apart from some 'quality' newspapers and programmes, standards of taste and decency have sunk to 'rock bottom'. God, the Bible, theology and the world-to-come are alluded to in the cheap journals and on the cheap channels only as subjects of jest and derision. Sport and entertainment (the latter often of a very dubious character) command the interest of at least 95 per cent of society in our sick Western society. If ever there was an age which appeared unready for Puritan reprinting, this is it!

But the wonderful truth is that our modern world, with all its love of superficiality and with all its contempt of spirituality, is witnessing – wonderful as it is to relate! – a worldwide resurgence of interest in the Puritans. This fact is as remarkable as it is exciting to all who love the religion of our Lord Jesus Christ. Good and evil are in our day springing up together side by side. It is a thing to be carefully noticed and to be prayed over.

———————

Stephen Charnock belonged to the third and last generation of the Puritan era and his writings stand easily on a level with the best of his contemporaries for profundity and edification. He was born in London in 1628, the son of a solicitor, and was descended from a family whose roots were in the county of Lancashire. (A motorway service station on the M6, it may be remembered, bears the name of Charnock Richard.) The researches of historians have not been able to discover anything about the boyhood of Charnock. We do know, however, that among many families of the middle classes at this time in the best areas of London there was a deep seriousness and thoughtfulness about the great issues of the Word of God. This was perhaps partly because times were grim. All could see the open conflict between King and Parliament which shortly afterwards led to the Civil War. But it was still more owing to the deeply serious religion of a large part of the populace in London at this time. Public sports were discouraged; the Lord's Day was kept strictly; family worship and Psalm-singing was commonly and extensively practised; church services were crowded. 'You might walk the streets on the evening of the Lord's Day without seeing an idle person, or hearing anything but the voice of prayer or praise from churches or private houses'. So wrote Daniel Neal in his *History of the Puritans*. In such an atmosphere Stephen Charnock passed the years of his boyhood.

Deeply interested in godly education, as all Puritans typically were, Charnock entered Emmanuel College, Cambridge in 1642. He was one of about two hundred students attending Emmanuel. This was the 'Puritan College' whose founder, Sir Walter Mildmay, had described it to Queen Elizabeth I as 'an acorn which, when it becomes an oak, God alone knows what will be the fruit thereof'. In the following years it was to breed large numbers of learned and influential scholars of whom Charnock was to be one of the most honourable.

A glance at events in the broader field at this time may help us to appreciate the sense of urgency which motivated men of Charnock's type to devote their lives to increasing labour and service for God. On the continent The Thirty Years' War was raging between 1618-1648. In the New World the Puritan colonies of Massachusetts and Connecticut, begun as recently as 1620, had grown to some thousands of persons who had been ready to leave their native shores in England to enjoy freedom of religion. In 1641 the Irish under O'Neill massacred 200,000 Protestants. This fearful event stirred the three kingdoms with alarm and indignation. Wherever one looked, religious and theological questions were the ones which moved men most at that time.

Charnock's lifelong habits of diligent study were well formed during his Cambridge days. His writings make reference to the Church Fathers, to the Mediaeval Thomas Aquinas and to a large number of Reformed theologians. He was fully versed in the writings of Calvin and other Reformers and he knew the works of Amyraut, Daille, Turretine, Zanchius and very many others, including the High Church Anglican writers of his own day.

We must, however, assert that he subjected all books to the supreme test of Holy Scripture. For Charnock, the Bible was the Word of God and the ultimate standard by which all opinions are to be tested and all human writings evaluated. Puritanism was nothing else than the application of the Bible to all life and thought with the aim of living to the glory of God.

Charnock's early ministerial career is not easy to trace now but it evidently began in Southwark, a district of London. After this brief experience of preaching (although not as a parish minister probably, but as a tutor or chaplain in a private family) he went to Oxford University for further study. Here he attached himself to a church 'gathered from among the scholars' whose minister was the eminent Dr Thomas Goodwin. At this time, it must be understood, Oliver Cromwell, the Lord Protector, was university chancellor at Oxford and the theologian Dr John Owen vice-chancellor. Both Cromwell and Owen were across in Ireland attending to what was even in those days a thorny political and religious situation.

In 1655 Oliver Cromwell sent his ablest son, Lord Harry Cromwell, to Ireland to keep an eye on affairs of state, and among the chaplains sent over with Lord Harry was Stephen Charnock. Here began, in Dublin, the most fruitful period of his ministry. For the next five years or so down probably to the Restoration of 1660 he preached to distinguished audiences who listened to him with great appreciation.

Preaching was Charnock's outstanding gift and his powers were at their height in this period of his life when he was in Dublin. His preparation was extensive. He spent most of his time in his study, and even when he took a walk out of doors he would stop from time to time to make jottings of ideas from the Scriptures which would occur to his mind – a regular Puritan practice.

In his delivery of the sermon itself at this time, Charnock used no notes but spoke extemporaneously. Considering the condensed nature of his thought as it is known to us from his written discourses, this must have made immense demands upon his memory. In later years this gift declined to some extent and he used a magnifying glass in the pulpit to read his notes. However, in these Dublin years he attracted and delighted his audiences with a spontaneous flow of thought and diction.

At the Restoration of Charles II in 1660 Charnock appears to have returned to England and, in those uncertain times, spent about fifteen years without a settled charge of his own. It was during this period that he was probably meditating on the great subject of the Attributes of God, which form the subject of the theological treatise for which he is best known.

In 1675 he was appointed joint pastor to Thomas Watson, formerly rector of St Stephen's, Walbrook in London. The congregation met in a building known as Crosby Hall. Here Charnock preached till his death on July 27th, 1680, being at that date only fifty-two years of age.

Clothed as he was with the modesty of deep godliness, Stephen Charnock published during his own lifetime nothing apart from one single sermon on the text Genesis 6:5. It bore only his initials, 'S.C.'.

After his death, however, his Oxford friends Richard Adams and Edward Veal prepared his manuscripts for the press. The first to appear was *A Discourse on Divine Providence* (1680). The voluminous and magisterial work *On the Existence and Attributes of God* first came out as a large folio in 1681–1682. It was followed by a further folio in 1683 containing discourses on Regeneration,

Reconciliation, the Lord's Supper and other important topics of theology. The book which is now in the reader's hands was first published, as far as the present writer can discover, in 1684. The best edition of his complete works is in 5 volumes in the Nichol's Series (1864).

The present edition of Charnock's *Christ Crucified* has been simplified by the explanation of many words and phrases not familiar to the average reader today. Even so, it is not light or easy reading because it speaks of things that are deeply spiritual and sublime. Yet the reader will be richly rewarded by taking the time and trouble to sit down to learn at the feet of Charnock about the glories of a crucified Saviour.

The editor has to confess that his labours in preparing this work for the press were so welcome and congenial to him that he blesses God for the privilege of ever having read the pages which make up this precious book.

If a reader wants cheap, easy and shallow thoughts, then let him stop now. This book is not a paddling pool for idlers but a wide and spacious sea for bold explorers to sail in.

Whoso wants to climb Jacob's ladder, to see angels, to touch the stars, to become intoxicated with heavenly emotions, to stand near the Gate of Gethsemane and to have his heart wrung with feelings of adoration at the goodness of God – let him read on.

And when he is finished let him not see Charnock or any man. But let him gaze on the face of Jesus and cry out through choking tears: 'I have seen the God-Man in his agonies. Surely this suffering was damnation taken lovingly for me. To Thee, O blessed Christ, I give my heart promptly and sincerely'.

Maurice Roberts

1

The Knowledge of Christ Crucified

For I determined not to know any thing among you, save
Jesus Christ, and him crucified.
1 Corinthians 2:2

The church of Corinth, to which the apostle directs this epistle, was a church as flourishing in gifts as any; yet as much crumbled into divisions as [it was] eminent in knowledge. A year and six months the apostle had been conversant among them, planting and watering, with expectation of a plentiful harvest; but no sooner had he turned his back, but [than] the devil steps in, and sows his tares. It was a church still, but divided; it had the evangelical doctrine, but too much choked with schismatical weeds.

Observe, the best churches are like the moon, not without their spots. The purest times had their imperfections; a pure state is not allowed to this, but [is] reserved for another world.

Church antiquity is a very unsafe rule. Other churches at some distance from the apostles were as subject to error as this. Pride and ambition were less like to keep out of them than out of Christ's family. Had the history of this church's practices and tenets, without this corrective epistle of the apostle been transmitted to after-ages, they would have been used as a pattern; not the church, but scripture authority, is to be followed. [The Church] Fathers must not be preferred before apostles; church practices are no patterns, but [only] as they are parallel to the grand and unerring rule [of Scripture].

The apostle, laying to heart the contentions among the Corinthians, draws up the whole doctrine which he had before preached unto them, into a short epitome [summary]. He first declares the manner of his first carriage [behaviour] among them: 'And I, brethren, when I came to you, not with excellency of speech, or of wisdom, declaring unto you the testimony of God' (v. 1).

To come with man's wisdom would detract from the strength and excellency of the word, which, as the sun, shines best with its own beams. The Spirit's eloquence is most piercing and demonstrative, and quickly convinceth a man by its own evidence. Carnal wisdom charms the ear, but this strikes the heart.

Man's wisdom detracts from the glory of God, who is more honoured by the simplicity of the gospel, than luxuriances of wit. It was his honour, by the doctrine of a crucified Saviour, to nonplus [confound] the wisdom of the world; and the glory of his wisdom as well as strength, to confound by impotent and weak men the power of Satan, which so long had possessed the hearts of the Corinthians.

It would be an argument of hypocrisy to use any other arguments than [ones that are] divine. Men in this would but seek themselves, not God's glory. It would be pride to think that their fancies could be more prevalent than evangelical reason; and therefore the apostle would do nothing but endeavour to set out Christ in his own colours, as he hung upon the cross, that their souls might be captivated to the obedience of a crucified Lord.

I determined. I judged it most convenient for me, most profitable for you. It was a resolution taken up deliberately. It was not for want of the knowledge of those principles which are cried up [praised] in the world for true wisdom. I understand them as well as others; but what things I counted gain before, I now count loss, for the excellency of the knowledge of Christ, and think it not worth the while and pains to make much inquiry about them.

To know nothing, to believe nothing, to approve of nothing, to make known nothing.

Not your *traditions*, which have for themselves the plea of a venerable antiquity, and have been handed to you from your ancestors. What I chiefly determine to know is as ancient as the oldest of those mysteries you so much admire, even the 'Lamb slain from the foundation of the world'.

Not your *philosophical wisdom*, so much admired by you and [by] the rest of the world. I come not to teach you a doctrine from Athens, but from Jerusalem, and not so much from Jerusalem, as from heaven. I come to declare him in whom are hid all the treasures of wisdom and knowledge.

Not your *poets*, wherein the chief mysteries of your religion are couched. I come to teach him to you, whom your sibyls [witches] and their prophetic writings pointed at long ago.

Nor your *mysterious oracles*, which had so long deluded the world; but I come to declare him by whose death they were silenced.

But Jesus Christ, and him crucified. Christ, in the Deity and glory of his person, but also as crucified, in the ignominy of his passion, and the advantages of his office.

This is the sum of the gospel, and contains all the riches of it. Paul was so much taken with Christ, that nothing sweeter than Jesus could drop from his lips and pen. It is observed that he hath the word 'Jesus' five hundred times in his epistles.

Others understand it thus: I will know nothing but Jesus Christ, though he were crucified; I will boast of him, whom others despise.

Among you: you Corinthians, though learned, though rich, I would not know any thing else among you than Christ, who is the wisdom of God, and the treasures of God.

Observe:

1. All human wisdom must be denied, when it comes in competition with the doctrine of Christ.

2. Christ and his death is the choicest subject for the wisest ear.

3. As all Christ, so especially his death, is the object of faith.

4. As all of Christ, so more especially his death in all the mysteries of it, ought to be the main subject of a Christian's study and knowledge.

Doctrine, For the last, AS ALL OF CHRIST, SO MORE ESPECIALLY HIS DEATH IN ALL THE MYSTERIES OF IT, OUGHT TO BE THE PRINCIPAL SUBJECT OF A CHRISTIAN'S STUDY AND KNOWLEDGE.

This is the honour of the gospel, and therefore the preaching of the gospel is called the preaching of the cross (1 Cor. 1:18) which should be considered by us: (1) in the first spring [origin]; (2) in the person suffering; (3) in the fruits of it.

1. In the first spring [origin]. His death was ordered by God Peter, as the president of the apostles, delivers it as the sense of the whole college of apostles then present. He was 'delivered by the determinate counsel and foreknowledge of God' (Acts 2:23).

It was decreed and enacted in heaven, resolved before time, though done in the fullness of time. Therefore Christ is called 'the Lamb slain from before the foundation of the world': determinately, in the counsel and decree of God; promissorily, in the promise and word of God passed to Adam after the Fall; typically, in sacrifices which were settled immediately upon that promise of redemption; efficaciously, in regard of the merit of it, applied by God to believers, before the actual suffering. He was made sin, not by us, not only by himself and his own will, but by God's ordination; 'he hath made him to be sin for us' (2 Cor. 5:21) by a divine statute; that is, he was ordained to be put into the state and condition of a sinner in our stead; not into the practical and experimental state of sin, but the penal state of a sinner, to be a sacrifice for it, not to be polluted with it.

Indeed, had not God appointed it, it had not been meritorious; for the merit was not absolute for us, but according to the covenant and condition. It was capable of meriting, because of the worth and dignity of the person, but not actually meritorious for us, but upon the covenant transacted between the Father and the Son; that it should be performed by him for us, and accepted by the Father for us, and applied by the Spirit to us.

And as it was appointed by God, it was:

1. An act of his sovereignty

Suppose God might have pardoned sin, and recovered man by his own absolute prerogative, had not his word been passed [if God had not said] that, in case of man's transgression, he should die the death. As a word created the earth, and cast it into such a beautiful frame and order, so by one word he might have restored man, and set him upon his former stock, and have for ever kept him from falling again, as he did the standing angels from ever sinning. Yet God chooseth this way, and is pleased with no other contrivance but this, and in a way of sovereignty he culls out his Son to be a sacrifice; and the Son, putting himself into the state of a Surety and Redeemer, is said to have a command given him on the part of God as a Sovereign: '[A]s the Father gave me commandment, even so I do' (John 14:31), and received by him as a subject (John 10:18), and God owns him as his servant (Isa. 42:1). So he took upon him 'the form of a servant' (Phil. 2:7), that is, the badge and livery of a servant; and the whole business he came upon, from his first breath to his last gasp, is called the will of God; and at the upshot he pleads his own obedience in finishing 'the work which though gavest me to do' as the ground of his expectations, and the glory promised him (John 17:4).

2. An act of the choicest love

God at the creation beheld man, a goodly frame of his own rearing, adorned with his own image, beautified with his graces, embellished with holiness and righteousness, and furnished with a power to stand. Afterwards God beheld him ungratefully (rebelling against his Sovereign, invading God's rights), and contemning God's goodness, forfeiting his own privileges, courting his ruin, and sinking into misery. So blinded is his mind, as not to be able to find out a way for his own recovery. So perverse is his will, that instead of craving pardon of his Judge, he flies from him, and when his flight would not advantage him, he stands upon his own defence, and extenuates his crime; thus adding one provocation to another, as if he had an ambition to harden the heart of God against him, and render himself irrecoverably miserable. God so overlooks these, as in immense love and grace to settle a way for man's recovery, without giving any dissatisfaction to his justice, so strongly engaged for the punishment of the offence. And rather than this notorious rebel and prodigious apostate should perish according to his desert, God would transfer the punishment (which he could not remit without a violation of his truth, and an injury to his righteousness) upon a person equal to himself, most beloved by him, his delight from eternity, and infinitely dearer to him than any thing in heaven or earth.

Herein was the emphasis of divine love to us, that he 'sent his Son to be the propitiation for our sins' (1 John 4:10). It was love that he would restore man after the Fall; there was no more necessity of doing this than of creating the world. As it added nothing to the happiness of God, so the want of it had detracted nothing from it. There was no more absolute necessity of setting up man again after his break-ing than of a new repair of the world after the destructive deluge. But that he might wind up his love to the highest pitch, he would not only restore man, but rather than let him lie in his deserved misery, would punish his own Son, to secure man from it. It was purely his grace which was the cause that his Son 'should taste death for every man' (Heb. 2:9).

3. An act of justice

As his love to us proposed it, and Christ, out of his affection to the honour of the Father and our welfare, accepted it, and was willing to undertake for us, and interpose between us and divine wrath, to stand in our stead and bear our sins, so it was then an act of justice to inflict. For God, being the Governor of the world, the great Lawgiver, righteously exacting obedience from his rational creature, upon the transgression of his law becomes a Judge, and his justice as a Ruler demands the punishment due for the transgression to be inflicted upon the offender. To preserve the rights of justice, and to give a contenting answer to the cry of mercy; to wipe off, as I may say, the tears of one, and smooth the frowns of the other, 'God lays our iniquity upon Christ' (Isa. 53:6). Christ takes the punishment upon himself, to bear our sins in his own body on the tree, and becomes responsible for our transgressions. And though he never sinned, nor stood indebted to God in his own person, yet, becoming our Surety, and being made under the law, putting himself in subjection to the law, and standing in our stead, he put himself also under the obligations of it to punishment. And thus the weight of the whole punishment due to man was laid upon Christ by God as a just Judge. That which he could not have from the debtors, he might have from the Surety, who had put himself under that obligation of payment and so was bound to undergo all those curses the law might have inflicted upon us; and pursuant to [in pursuance of] this obligation, God imputed our iniquities to him and punished them in him.

2. Consider the person suffering

In regard of his dignity

The Son of God became man, the Lord of glory emptied himself. It was the Lord of angels that took upon him the nature of a servant; the Lord of life shed his blood. It was the Son of God who stooped down infinitely below himself into our nature, to be a sacrifice for our redemption; he that was greater than heaven became meaner than a worm.

The willingness of his suffering

He, being equal with the Father, could not be commanded to undertake this. He willingly consented, and willingly accomplished it. He was not driven, as the legal sacrifices were, to the altar. His enemies were not so desirous to make him a sufferer, as he himself was straitened till he was a sufferer (Luke 12:50). The cup was as willingly drunk by him, as it was tempered by God; and his enemies did not so maliciously put him to shame, as he joyfully endured it (Heb. 12:2). The desire that the cup might pass from him was the struggle of his human nature, not an unwillingness in his person, or a repenting of his undertaking this office. It was a natural motion, evidencing the truth of his humanity, and the greatness of what he was to suffer.

The greatness of his suffering

His death has all the ingredients of bitterness in it. It was a grievous punishment, because the holiness of God would not have been so manifested in a light one.

(1) Ignominious. It was a death for slaves and malefactors; for slaves whose condition rendered them most despicable, and for malefactors whose actions had rendered them most abominable. The Lord of heaven endured the punishment of a slave, and was numbered among transgressors. It is called 'shame' (Heb. 12:2). Each suffering was sharpened with shame; he was buffeted, spit upon, wounded in his good name, accounted as impostor, the most odious terms of 'blasphemer', 'Beelzebub's agent', etc., were put upon the Son of God.

(2) Cruel and sharp: lingering, not sudden; from his scourging by Pilate to his death was six hours, all that while in much torture; he suffered from heaven, earth, hell, in his body, in his soul.

(3) Accursed. As under God's blessing, all blessings are included, so under the notion of a curse, all punishment is contained: 'being made a curse for us' (Gal. 3:13). This must be something more dreadful than a bare outward pain or bodily punishment; Christ wanted not courage to support that, as well as the most valiant martyr; he bore the beginnings of it till he saw a black cloud between his Father and himself. This made him cry out, 'My God, my God', etc. The agonies of Christ were more than the sufferings of all the martyrs, and all men in the world, since God laid upon him the sins of the whole world.

3. Consider the fruits of his death, which will render it worth our study

The appeasing the wrath of God for us
God was willing to be appeased (hence the sending of Christ is everywhere in scripture ascribed to the love and grace of God); but his justice was not actually appeased till the death of Christ. As a merciful God, he pitied us; but as a holy God, he could not but hate our transgression; as a God of truth, he could not but fulfil his own threatening; as a God of justice, he must avenge himself for the offence against him. He gave Christ as a God of mercy, and required satisfaction as a God of justice. 'God hath set forth to be a propitiation ... that he might be just' (Rom. 3:25, 26). His mercy rendered him placable, but his righteousness hindered the actual forgiveness. He had a kindness for man, but could not have a kindness for his sin; he had mercy for

his creature to free him, but no mercy for his transgression to let that go unpunished. That justice, whereby he can no more absolve the guilty than condemn the innocent, was an obstacle to the full issues of his mercy.

But when an offering for sin was made by an infinite person (our near kinsman who had a right of redemption), there was no plea in justice against it, since the sacrifice was complete; no plea in divine veracity, since the penalty was suffered; no plea in divine holiness, since that was infinitely manifested; no bar to mercy's coming, smiling upon the world. The wrath of God was appeased upon the death of the Redeemer; and this reconciliation is actually applied upon the acceptance of the believer. If God had not been placable, he had never [would never have] accepted a substitute; and if he had not been appeased, he had never [would never have] raised this substitute after his passion, nor ever held out his hand of grace to invite us to be reconciled to him. There is nothing now remains to be done, but our consenting to those terms upon which he offers us the actual enjoyment of it.

This crucified Redeemer only was able to effect this work. He was an infinite person, consisting of a divine and a human nature: the union of the one gave value to the suffering of the other. The word of God was past in his threatening; his justice would demand its right of his veracity; a sacrifice there must be, to repair the honour of God by bearing the penalty of the law, which could not be done by the strength and holiness of any creature. All the created force in the earth, and the strongest force of the angelic nature, were too feeble for so great a task. Justice must have satisfaction; the sinner could not give it without suffering eternal punishment. Jesus then puts himself into our place, to free us from the arrest of justice, and bear those strokes, which, by virtue of the law, wrath had prepared for us. The dignity of his person puts a value upon his punishment, and renders it acceptable for us, it being a death superior in virtue to the death of worlds; it was a death which justice required, and at the sight of it justice was so calmed, that the sharp revenging sword drops out of its hand.

God hath smelt in it so sweet a savour that it hath fully pleased him. He can now pardon the sins of believers with the glory of his righteousness as well as of his grace. He can legally justify a repenting sinner. God hath been served in the passion of the Redeemer, his justice and holiness were glorified, and the law accomplished, the honour of God is preserved, and the author of the law righted, the justice of God sweetened. By this propitiation for sin, God is rendered propitious to guilty man, and stretches out his arms of love, instead of brandishing his sword of vengeance.

The ancient [Old Testament] believers lived in the expectation of this, but they beheld not the consummation of it; they thirsted for it, but were not satisfied with it, till the fullness of time. It solely depended upon the passion of Christ; it is by the cross that God is reconciled, and all enmity slain (Eph. 2:14). He was then wounded for our iniquities, and being cast into the furnace of divine wrath, quenched the flames; as Jonah the type, who being cast into the raging sea quelled the storm. He bore our sins by bearing the wrath due to them, and satisfied justice by suffering its strokes. It could not stand with [would not be consistent with] that justice to punish him, if he were not placed in our stead to be the mark and butt of that justice for us and our sins. Doth not then a crucified Christ deserve to be known and studied by every one of us, who hath done that upon the cross, which the holy law, sacrifices divinely instituted, the blessed angels, the purity and strength of universal nature, had never [would never have] been able to effect? He hath expiated our sins, and by his blood hath secured us from the sword of divine vengeance, if we refuse not the atonement he hath made.

Silencing the law

Christ crucified, by satisfying the justice of God, brake the thunders of the law and dissolved the frame of all its anathemas. Being made a curse for us, he hath redeemed us from the curse of the law (Gal. 3:13), that is, from the sentence of the Law-giver, denounced in his law against the transgressors of it. So that now '[t]here is therefore no condemnation to them which are in Christ Jesus' (Rom. 8:1) because they are 'dead to the law by the body of Christ' (Rom. 7:4). By the body of Christ as slain and raised again, this handwriting of ordinances, which was contrary to us, is taken out of the way by God, being nailed to his cross (Col. 2:14). He hath abolished the obligation of the moral law as to any condemning power, it being the custom to cancel bonds anciently by piercing the writing with a nail. The ceremonial law was abolished in every regard, since the substance of it was come, and that which it tended to was accomplished; and so one understands, 'having spoiled principalities and powers, he made a shew of them openly' (v. 15), of the ceremonies of the law, called 'principalities and powers' in regard of the divine authority whereby they were instituted. These he spoiled, as the word signifies, unclothing or unstripping, he unveiled them, and showed them to be misty figures that were accomplished in his own person. The flower falls when the fruit comes to appear; grace and truth came by Jesus Christ, grace to obey the precepts, and truth to take away the types.

But it is also meant of the condemning power of the moral law, which was nullified by the death of Christ, who, upon his cross sealing another covenant, repealed the former. The settling a new covenant implies the dissolution of the old. That was nailed to his cross which was contrary to us, a law that was a charge against us, and by virtue whereof we are sued; and this was the law as sentencing us to death, which was pierced and torn by those nails, that did discover that debt, and denounce the sentence, which cannot be meant so properly of the ceremonial, as the moral law. The ceremonial law of sacrifices was the gospel in shadows, and appointed for the relief of men, and as a ground whereon to exercise their faith till the appearance of the substance, and therefore cannot be said to be contrary to us, but an amicable discovery, that we were to have that relief in another, which we wanted in ourselves, and that we were to be freed from the sentence of death by some grand sacrifice represented by those sacrifices of animals.

Besides, the apostle writes this as a cordial, issuing out of the blood of Christ to the Gentile Colossians, who never were under the obligation of the ceremonial law, that being appropriated to the Jews. The apostle brings it to back [support] his assertion that their trespasses were forgiven. The argument had been of no use to the Gentiles, who sinned not against the ceremonial law, but the moral law; and if one only had been cancelled, and not the other, the Jews themselves, whose offences were most against the moral law, had [would have] had little or no comfort in having the fewest of their sins forgiven. Our Saviour died by the power and force of the moral law; that brought him to the cross, for the fulfilling it in its penalty, as well as he had done in his life by his obedience; and he receiving the full execution of its sentence upon himself on the cross, as a substitute in our place, nullified that sentence as to any force upon those who believe in him. The plea against it is, that it hath already been executed, though not upon our persons, yet upon our Surety; so that being nailed to his cross, the virtue of his cross must cease, before the killing power of the law can revive. This crucified Christ, who disarmed the law of its thunders, defaced the obligation of it as a covenant, and, as it were, ground the stones upon which it was written to powder, is worth our exact knowledge and studious inquiry.

Upon this must follow the removal of guilt
If God the Judge of the world be appeased and satisfied, and the law, upon which our accusation is grounded and which is the testimony of our debt, be cancelled, the removal of our guilt must necessarily follow. And this forgiveness of sin is the chief and principal part of our redemption, and ascribed to his blood as the procuring cause: 'In whom we have redemption through his blood, the forgiveness of sins' (Eph. 1:7). He bearing [Since he has borne] our sins in his own body on the tree, there necessarily follows a discharge of every believer from them. The payment made by the Surety is a discharge of the principal debtor from the pursuit of the creditor. As he took away the curse from us by being made a curse, so he took away sin from us by being made sin for us. The taking away of the sins of the world was the great end [purpose] of his coming.

There had been no need of his assuming our nature, and exposing himself to such miseries for our relief, had we been only in a simple misery, for then we might have been rescued by his strength. But, being in a *sinful* misery, we could not be relieved but by his sacrifice to remove our guilt, as well as by his strength to draw us out of our gulf [misery]. Our sin was a bar upon the treasures of divine blessings; this must be removed before those could be opened for us, and could not righteously be removed by bare power, but by a full payment and satisfaction of the debt. It is a violent oppression to free a creditor from the hands of a debtor by force; it is righteous only when it is by legal payment.

Well then, 'For he hath made him to be sin for us' (2 Cor. 5:21), and that is in his death upon the cross. To what end? That sin might remain in its guilt upon us? No, for him to be made sin, and that by God, without respect to the taking away of sin, had [would have] been inconsistent with the wisdom and righteousness of God. The justice of God would not permit him to take our debt of [from] another, and yet to charge it upon ourselves. 'For he hath made him to be sin for us, who knew no sin; that we might be made the righteousness of God in him.' He was made sin that we might be counted without sin by the imputation of the righteousness of the Mediator to us, as if it were our own; that as he represented our persons and bore our penalty, we might likewise receive the advantages of his righteousness for the acquittal of our debts, the sin of our nature and the sin of our persons, the removal of the guilt contracted by Adam and imputed to us, and the guilt contracted by ourselves. For it is of 'many offences unto justification' (Rom. 5:16).

He was the true person figured by the scapegoat that took away our sins and carried them into a land of forgetfulness, where none dwells to take notice of them and censure us to death for the crimes. Is not then this crucified

Christ worth the knowing, who took such heavy burdens upon his own shoulders that they might not oppress ours, and suffered as a victim in the place of our guilty persons, to obtain an eternal redemption for us (Heb. 9:14)? He that gives so great a ransom for us, as that of his life and precious blood, rather than we should remain in our chains, deserves the choicest place in our understanding as well as affections. Were it a bare deliverance, it would challenge this. But he is said not only to deliver us – which speaks power, but to redeem us – which speaks price and a buying what was past into the possession of another; a payment of that which we were never able to pay.

The conquest of Satan

The empire [which] the devil exercised over man did not arise from any dignity in his person or any right he had to man in himself. But it was first founded on sin, and granted to Satan by the justice of God, and was not the power of a prince, but of an executioner. Had not sin first opened the door, his venom could not have infected us nor his power have hurt us. He could never have been our accuser without some matter of charge from us: nor ever have been our executioner, had we not fallen under the hands of divine justice. His power is erected upon our crimes, whereby he becomes the minister of divine vengeance.

But a crucified Christ hath bruised the head of this old serpent and wounded the prince of this world! He hath displaced him from his power, snatched from him the ground of his indictments, by cancelling the law upon which his accusations are founded; and despoiled him of his office, by satisfying divine justice, which conferred an authority upon him of executing divine vengeance; 'the accuser of our brethren is cast down' (Rev. 12:10) and 'destroy[ed] him that had the power of death', and that through his own death (Heb. 2:14, 15).

That the devil had not a total power over Adam, after the Fall, proceeded from the intervention of this Surety, and the absolute credit of his future victory over him. Yet that promise, that the serpent's head should be bruised, did not, through the weakness of their faith and the long delay of performance, preserve them from the fear of death; notwithstanding that [promise], they were all their life-time subject to bondage; for since the devil's empire was reared upon the ruins of men by sin, he could continually object to them that their sins were not expiated, that death remained as a punishment of sin. But the cross of Christ hath disarmed him of this weapon; his grand plea, whereby he kept men in a servile fear, is completely answered.

In bruising our Saviour's heel by the death on the cross, he felt a fatal blow on his head, his conqueror got above him out of his reach, without any hope left in him to touch his heel again. The devil's right was legally taken from him by Christ's death on the cross; the foundation of his authority, namely sin, was taken away. He was destroyed (that is the apostle's expression) not in his person, but in his authority; he was irrecoverably expelled from his dominion which he had by his false oracles usurped over the world (John 12:31). It is by this crucified Christ that we are more than conquerors over him. And should we not know this crucified Christ, who hath weakened the venom of the serpent, broke the force of the tempter, vanquished him on the cross by the merit of his blood, and conquers him in us by the efficacy of his Spirit?

Sanctification is another fruit of the cross of Christ

To be delivered from the guilt of sin, that bound us over to punishment, had [would have] been a great favour; but it would not have been a perfect favour, without being delivered from the venom of sin that had infected our nature. Though God willed man good by a love of good will, yet he could not delight in man with a love of complacency if the contagion and filth of sin had deformed and sullied our souls as much as before. If our guilt were only removed, we had been [would have] freed from punishment; but without restoring the divine image, we had not [would not have] been fit for any converse [conversation] with God. It was necessary that our souls should be washed, and our faculties put into a state to serve in some measure the glory of God and the end [purpose] of our creation.

God would have seemed to deny his own holiness if he had regarded only the reverence of his justice, by appointing a sacrifice for atonement, and not consulted the honour of the other, by renewing his image in the nature of man. But this is purchased by the death of Christ; '[H]e that came by water and blood' (1 John 5:6), by blood to expiate our sins, and by water to purify our souls, answerable to the Jewish state wherein it was typified, where there were sacrifices for guilt and washings for filth.

These two things come to us by the death of Christ, the remitting our crime and the removing of our spot [defilement]. He gave himself that he might save us (Eph. 5:25; Titus 2:14); when he came to purchase the blessings we had forfeited, he would not omit this, which was one of the chief. By him the conscience is purged from dead works, from sin which brought death and, being worse than a pollution by a dead body, hindered us from access to God, as that did from an entrance into the temple. He hath broken our chains, as well as blotted out our crimes; healed our natures, as well as procured our pardon; purchased our regeneration, as well as remission. It is by his cross that the old man, which had incorporated himself with our souls, is crucified (Rom. 6:6). By this he gained the power of sending a saving Spirit, which had not [who would not have] entered into our souls, had not Christ's blood flowed out of his veins. The effusion of this blood was the cause of the effusion of the Spirit; it was shed upon us through Christ alone.

He hath, by suffering for sin on the cross, rendered it a detestable thing, and showed how dreadful sin is that it could not receive its fatal wound without a wound first in the heart of the Son of God. This is the most powerful motive to quicken us to a hatred of sin and a love of holiness; and his life is the most illustrious pattern; but all this had been of little efficacy to us, had not the water of the Spirit flowed out from the Rock, when it was struck, to cleanse the filthiness of our souls. This is given, upon the account of his death, to believers to purify their hearts from the mud of the world and to form them to a new life for the honour of God; and it is not denied to those who will ask, and seek, and knock (Luke 11:13).

Had Christ only purchased remission [forgiveness] without sanctification, it had not been [would not have been] for the honour of God's holiness, nor would our condition have been elevated; heaven had been no [would not have been the] place for defilements or slaves. It was necessary the filth of sin should be removed, the dominion of sin be abolished, that we might as holy persons approach to God and as free men converse [speak] with him. Is not a crucified Christ then worth the knowing, who hath not only destroyed Satan our enemy without us, but can destroy sin our enemy within us? As he hath snatched us from punishment by expiating our sins, so he can bring us to communion with God, by razing [eradicating] evil habits out of our hearts; without this latter, we are not capable of enjoying a complete benefit by the former.

Opening heaven for us

What is this life but a wallowing in a sink, a converse in the dregs [living in the filth] of the creation, in an earth polluted by the sin of man, wherein we every day behold fresh affronts of [insults offered to] God, and find motions [sinful tendencies] in us dishonourable to ourselves? But Christ by his death hath provided a better place than this, yea, a place more glorious than Adam's Paradise which was designed for our habitation by the first creation. A place, not only built by the word of God, but cemented and prepared by the blood of Christ. By the law against sin, we were to have our bodies reduced to dust, and our souls lie under the sentence of the wrath of God. But our crucified Saviour hath purchased the redemption of our body, to be evidenced by a resurrection (Rom. 8:23) and a standing security of our souls in a place of bliss, to which believers shall have a real ascent, and in which they shall have a local residence, which is called the purchased possession.

As Adam brought in the empire of death, so Christ hath brought in the empire of life (Rom. 5:17). He hath not purchased for us a paradisiacal life [a life in an earthly paradise] or restored us to the mutable state wherein Adam was created; he hath not linked us for ever to the earth and the use of the creatures for our support. He hath purchased for us an eternal life and prepared for us eternal mansions; not only to have the company of men, or the society of the blessed angels, but to be blessed with the vision of God, to reside in the same place where his glorified person is adored by the happy spirits, to live with him (Rom. 6:8); a life, wherein our understandings shall be freed from mists, our wills from spots [blemishes] and our affections from disorder. We lost a paradise by sin, and have gained a heaven by the cross. And should not this crucified Christ be studied, who hath settled the regions above for our reception and procured an entrance into that place, which justice by reason of our sin had else made for ever inaccessible to us?

I might mention more: such as, the establishment of the covenant, access to God, perseverance and the conquest of the world.

Uses [ways in which we may apply this teaching]:

1. Let us be thankful to God for a crucified Redeemer.
There is nothing in heaven or earth such an amazing wonder as this; nothing can vie [compete] with it for excellence. All love and thankfulness is due to God, who hath given us his Son, not only to live but to die for us a death so shameful, a death so accursed, a death so sharp, that we might be repossessed of the happiness we had lost. All love and thankfulness is due to Christ who did not pay a small sum for us as our Surety, but bowed his soul to death to raise us to life, and was numbered among transgressors that we might have a room among the blessed. Our crimes merited our sufferings, but his own mercy made him a sufferer for us; for us he sweat [sweated] those drops of blood, for us he trod the wine-press alone; for us he assuaged [quenched] the rigour [severity] of divine justice, for us, who were not

only miserable but offending creatures, and overwhelmed with more sins to be hated than with misery to be pitied. He [Christ] was crucified for us by his love, though we deserved to die by his power, and has laid the highest obligation upon us though we had laid the highest offences upon him.

This death is the ground of all our good. Whatever we have is a fruit that grew upon the cross. Had he not suffered, we had [would have] been rejected for ever from the throne of God; salvation had [would have] never appeared, but by those groans and agonies. By this alone was God pleased and our souls for ever made happy. Without it, he had [would have] been for ever displeased with us. We had [would have] been odious and abominable in his sight and could never have seen his face. Nothing is such an evidence of his love as his cross. The miracles he wrought and the cures he performed in the time of his life were nothing to the kindness of his death, wherein he was willing to be accounted worse than a murderer in his punishment that he might thereby effect our deliverance. If he had given us the riches of this world and – greater still – had he given us the honour of angels and made us barons of heaven, without exposing himself to the cross to accomplish it, it had [would have] been a testimony of his affection, but destitute of so endearing an emphasis. The manner of procuring is more than a bare kindness in bestowing it; he testified his resolution not only to give us glory but to give it us whatsoever it should cost him, and would stick at nothing rather than we should want [lack] it. The angels in heaven in their glistering [glittering] lustre are the monuments of his liberality, but not of so supreme an affection as is engraven on the body of his cross.

2. Let us delight in the knowledge of Christ crucified and be often in the thought and study of him.

Study Christ, not only as living but [also] dying, not [only] as breathing in our air but [also] suffering in our stead; know him as a victim which [for this] is the way to know him as a conqueror. Christ crucified is the great object of faith. All the passages of his life, from his nativity to his death, are passed over in the creed without reciting because, though they are things to be believed, yet the belief of them is not sufficient without the belief of the cross. In that alone was our redemption wrought. Had he only lived, he had not been [would not have been] a Saviour. If our faith stop in [is restricted to] his life and do [does] not fasten upon his blood, it will not be a justifying faith. His miracles, which prepared the world for his doctrine; his holiness, which fitted himself for his suffering, had [would have] been insufficient for us without the addition of the cross. Without this, we had [would have] been under the demerit of our crimes, the venom of our natures, the slavery of our sins and the tyranny of the devil. Without this, we should for ever have had God for our enemy and Satan for our executioner; without this, we had laid [should have laid] groaning under the punishment of our transgressions and despaired of any smile from heaven. It was this death which as a sacrifice appeased God and as a price redeemed us; nothing is so strong to encourage us; nothing so powerful to purify us; how can we be without thinking [how can we fail to think] of it? The world we live in had [would have] fallen upon our heads, had it not been upheld by the pillar of the cross, had not Christ stepped in and promised a satisfaction for the sin of man. By this all things consist. [There is] not a blessing we enjoy but may put us in mind of it. They were all forfeited by our sins but merited by his precious blood. If we study it well, we shall be sensible [aware of] how God hated sin and loved a world; how much he would part with to restore a fallen creature. He showed an irresistible love to us, not to be overcome by a love to his own dear Son.

This will keep up life in [ensure there is life in] our repentance. We cannot look upon Christ crucified for us, for our guilt, and consider that we had deserved all that he suffered; and that he suffered not by our entreaty nor by any obligation from us but merely from his own love; but the meditation of this must needs melt us into sorrow. Should we not bleed [at heart] as often as we seriously thought of Christ's bleeding for us? You cannot see a malefactor led to execution for a notorious crime, but you have some detesting thoughts of the fact as well as some motions of pity to the person. A strong meditation on Christ will not only excite compassion for his sufferings, but a detestation of our sins and selves as the cause of them. It is a look upon Christ pierced that pierceth the soul (Zech. 12:10).

Would not this blood acquaint us that the malignity [evil] of sin was so great that it could not be blotted out by the blood of the whole creation? Would it not astonish us that none had strength enough to match it, but one equal with God? Would not such an astonishment break out into penitent reflections [repentant thoughts]? Would not the thoughts of this make us emulate the veil of the temple and be ashamed that it should outstrip us in rending, while our hearts remain unbroken? Should we not be confounded that a lifeless earth should shake in the time of his sufferings, while our reasonable souls stand immovable? Could any of the Israelites, that understood the nature and intent of sacrifices, be without some penitent motions [emotions] while they saw the innocent victim slain for their sin, not for any fault of its own? And should we be unmelted if we considered the cross, the punishment of *our* crimes, not *his*?

It will inspirit [inspire] our faith when we see his blood confirming an everlasting covenant, wherein God promises to be gracious. All the promises centred in the cross, received their life from his death, and are from thence reflected on us. Where can faith find a vigour, but in the royalties of mercy displayed in the satisfaction of justice? Where can it find a life but in the views of its proper object? When we behold a Christ crucified, how can we distrust God that hath in that, as a plain tablet, written this language 'that he will spare nothing for us, since he hath not spared the best he had'? What greater assurance can he give? Where is there any thing in heaven or earth that can be a greater judge of his [God's] affection [for us]?

This will animate us in our approaches to God. Not only a bare coming, but a boldness and confidence in coming to God was purchased by a crucified Christ (Heb. 10:19). God was before averse from [opposed to] man and man was unwilling to approach to God. Now God invites and man may come; man calls and God answers. What can be more encouraging than to consider that by his blood he hath made us kings and priests to God (Rev. 5:9, 10) to offer up sacrifices with a royal spirit, since the curse which should have fallen upon our heads has been borne by him? We should think of it every time we go to God in prayer. It was by this death the throne of God was opened. This will chase away that fear that disarms us of our vigour. It will compose our souls to offer up delight-ful petitions. It is in this only we see the face of God appeased towards us.

This will be a means to further us in progress towards holiness. An affection to sin, which cost the Redeemer of the world so dear, would be inconsistent with a sound knowledge and serious study of a crucified Saviour. We should see no charms in sin that may not be overcome by that ravishing love which bubbles up in every drop of the Redeemer's blood.

Can we, with lively thoughts of this, sin against so much tenderness, compassion, grace and the other perfections of God which sound so loud in our ears from the cross of Jesus? Shall we consider him hanging there to deliver us from hell and yet retain any spirit to walk in the way which leads thereto [i.e. to hell]? Shall we consider him upon the cross, unlocking the gates of heaven, and yet turn our backs upon that place he was so desirous to purchase for us and give us the possession of? Shall we see him groaning in our place and stead and dare to tell him, by our unworthy carriage [behaviour], that we regard him not and that he might have spared his pains?

It must be a miserable soul, worse than brutish, that can walk on in ways of enmity, with a sense of a crucified Christ in his mind. Could we then affect [love] that sin which appears so horrible in the doctrine of the cross? Can we take any pleasure in that which procured so much pain to our best Friend? Can we love that which hath brought a curse, better than him who bore the curse for us?

For want of this study of Christ crucified we walk on in sin, as if he suffered to purchase a licence for it rather than the destruction of it. The due consideration of this death would incline our wills to new desires and resolutions. It would stifle that luxury, ambition and worldliness which harass our souls. We should not dare to rush into any iniquity through the wounds of Christ. We should not, under a sense of his dying groans, cherish that for which he suffered. We should not do the works of darkness under the effusions of his blood, if we did in a serious posture set ourselves at the feet of his cross.

This will be the foundation of all comfort. What comfort can be wanting, when we can look upon Christ crucified as our Surety and look upon ourselves as crucified in him; when we can consider our sins as punished in him and ourselves accepted by virtue of his cross? It was not an angel which was crucified for us, but the Son of God; one of an equal dignity with the Father; one who shed blood enough to blot out the demerit of our crimes, were they more than could be numbered by all the angels of heaven, if all were made known to them. He was not crucified for a few, but for all sorts of offences. When we shall see judgments in the world, what comfort can we take without a knowledge and sense of a crucified Christ? What a horror is it for a condemned man to see the preparation of gibbets [gallows], halters [nooses] and executions? But when he shall see a propitiation made for him, the anger of the prince atoned, the law satisfied, and his condemnation changed into remission; all his former terrors vanish and a sweet and pleasing calm possesses him.

With this knowledge and sense, we shall not be much terrified at the approaches of death in our last gasps when we consider [death] itself gasping under the weight of the cross. The blood of Christ is as a balsam dropped upon the points of the arrows of death. That blood, by removing the guilt of sin, pulled out the sting of death. When we tremble under a sense of our sins, the terrors of the Judge and the curses of the law, let us look upon a crucified Christ, the remedy of all our miseries. His cross hath procured a crown, his passion hath expiated our transgression. His death hath disarmed the law, his blood hath washed a believer's soul. This death is the destruction of our enemies, the spring of our happiness, the eternal testimony of divine love. We have good reason, as well as the apostle, to determine with ourselves 'to know nothing but Jesus Christ, and especially him crucified'.

2

A Discourse on Christ our Passover

For even Christ our passover is sacrificed for us ...
1 Corinthians 5:7

These words are a reason for the apostle's exhortation to the Corinthians to cast out the incestuous person, in regard of the contagion, which might be, by so ill [bad] an example, dispersed to others, as leaven [yeast] spreads in vapours through the whole lump: 'Know ye not that a little leaven leaveneth the whole lump?' (v. 6). And having used this similitude of leaven, he pursues it in allusion to the custom of the Jews before the celebration of the passover, according to the command, to have no leaven found in their houses at that time, upon the penalty of being cut off from the congregation of Israel; and with respect to the true design of that ceremonial injunction [command of the ceremonial law], he exhorts the Corinthians to purge out the old leaven, namely, that person from their society, the lust from their hearts, every member of the old Adam, that they might be a new lump answering their holy and heavenly calling.

The reason of [for] this exhortation is in the words, 'For even Christ our passover is sacrificed for us' (v. 7), and by his death hath taken away the sin of the world. As the sacrifice of the paschal lamb represented the sacrifice of Christ, so the manner wherein the Israelites celebrated that solemnity with unleavened bread, represents the manner wherewith we ought to celebrate the death of the Redeemer of the world. As therefore our true passover, which is the Lord Jesus, hath been sacrificed for us, let us daily celebrate the memory of it in a manner worthy of so great a grace. As therefore the Jews abstained from all leaven in the time of the figure [symbol], let us not only abstain from, but purge out all things contrary to God, because for this end Christ was sacrificed for us. As the passover was a type of Christ, so the unleavened bread was a type of Christians, and of their innocence and purity of life. And that because you are unleavened by law, you ought to be so: for that is said in scripture sometimes to be in fact, which ought to be; as 'the priest's lips should keep knowledge' (Mal. 2:7), that is, ought to preserve knowledge. 'Purge out' is very emphatic and means 'Purge it out wholly, that nothing may be left in you, that you may be such as a new lump did figuratively signify'.

'Christ our passover.' The institution of this solemn figure [ceremony] is particularly set down (Exod. 12:3-5, etc.). It was appointed by God as a memorial both of the Israelites' slavery in Egypt and their deliverance from it. After they had been about two hundred years in that country, God, mindful of his promise, sets upon their delivery, and since all the former miracles had proved unsuccessful for the bending Pharaoh's heart to give the captives liberty to depart, God designs the slaying of the first-born of every

Egyptian family, and thereby sending the greatest strength of the nation to another world [i.e. to death]. Upon this occasion he orders the Israelites, by Moses, to slay the lamb on the fourteenth day of the first month (which answers to our March), and to sprinkle the posts of their doors with the blood, and to feast upon the flesh of it in their several families; and that night the angel comes, and mortally strikes every first-born, none escaping but those who observed this command of God, and had sprinkled their door posts with the blood of the slain lamb; every house besides being made that night a house of mourning. It was an earnest [foretaste] of the Israelites' deliverance and the Egyptians' calamity.

Observe:

(1) God's greatest mercies to his church are attended with the greatest plagues upon their enemies. The salvation of man is the destruction of sin and the devil. The passover was the salvation of Israel and the ruin of Egypt.

(2) God provides for the security of his people before he lays his wrathful hand upon their adversaries. He provided a Moses to conduct them, an ordinance to comfort and refresh them, before he shoots his arrows into the Egyptians' hearts. God settles this passover as a standing ordinance in the church; a feast throughout their generations, to be kept by an ordinance for ever (Exod. 12:14); so that it was not only a memorial of a past and temporal deliverance, but the type of a future and spiritual one. As all the sacrifices were types of what was to be performed in the fullness of time in the person of the Messiah, so this was a great and signal type, and had its truth, reality and efficacy in the death of the Redeemer.

57

'Christ the passover', that is, *the* paschal lamb. The lamb was called the passover; the sign for the thing signified by it. 'And they killed the passover' (2 Chron. 35:11), that is, the lamb; for the passover was properly the angel's passing over Israel, when he was sent as an executioner of God's wrath upon the Egyptians. So Matthew 26:17: 'Where wilt thou that we prepare for thee to eat the passover?', that is, the paschal lamb.

'Our passover': *our* paschal lamb. He is called God's lamb (John 1:29). God's in regard of the author, ours in regard of the end; God's lamb in regard of designation, ours in regard of acceptation [acceptance].

'Our passover.' Not only of the Jews but of the Gentiles; that was restrained to the Israelite nation, this extends in the offers of it to all, and belongs to all that are under the new administration of the covenant of grace.

'For us.' Not only for our good, but in our stead, to free us from eternal death, to purchase for us eternal life: sacrifices were substituted in the place of the transgressor, and received the stroke of death which his sin had merited. The title of the paschal lamb is given here to Christ, not only in regard of his meekness and innocence, but in regard of his being a sacrifice, whence he is called the lamb slain (Rev. 5:12), the 'lamb that redeems us by his blood' (1 Pet. 1:19).

Here we have: (1) a description of Christ in the type – passover; and (2) the end [aim] of his death. Three doctrines may be observed from the words

1. Christ is our Passover;

2. Christ is a Sacrifice;

3. Christ is a Sacrifice in our Stead.

Part 1: Christ is our Passover
In allusion to this, he is so often called a lamb, as also in allusion to the lambs offered in the daily sacrifice; but especially in relation to the paschal lamb which did more fully express both the nature of his sufferings and the design of his office. You do not therefore find him expressed in the New Testament by the name of any of those other animals which were figures of him in the Jewish sacrifices, but only by this of a lamb, as being more significant of the innocence of his person, the meekness of his nature, his sufficiency for his people, than any other.

(1) *The design of the passover was to set forth Christ.*
All the sacrifices, which were appointed by God as parts of worship, were designed to keep up the acknowledgment of the fall of man, his demerit by sin, and to support his faith in the promised Redeemer; for they being instituted not before the fall, but probably immediately after the first promise of the Seed of the woman, did all refer to that Seed promised, whose heel was to be bruised, as to the foundation of their institution; and being unable of themselves to purge the sin of a rational creature and the spiritual substance of the soul, they must refer to that which was only able to do it: 'Sacrifice and offering, and burnt offerings and offering for sin thou wouldest not, neither hadst pleasure therein ... Then said he, Lo, I come to do thy will' (Heb. 10:8-9). The will of God as manifested in the first draught and agreement in heaven, and shadowed in all the sacrifices under the law. When sacrifices of themselves were not, nor could be, grateful [welcome] to God, nor [could] the blood of an animal give a due compensation to an offended God for the sin of man, then said Christ, 'Lo, I come', as the

person represented by those pictures, as the body signified by those shadows.

All those institutions, not being designed for any virtue in themselves, but as notices of the intent [intention] of God, and the methods [which] he designed for taking away sin by the promised Seed. It was to be by blood and death, because this was the agreement between God and the Seed so promised. Therefore they were, in all those doleful spectacles of blood and slaughter, to look through that veil to the calamities the promised Seed should endure for taking away sin, and have a prospect [realisation] of the heinousness of sin, and the sharpness of the sufferings of the Messiah, in the groans and strugglings of those dying creatures [i.e. the lambs sacrificed]. So the design of this passover was ultimately to represent the Messiah to them, by whose blood they were to have a spiritual deliverance from sin and Satan, just as, by the blood of the lamb, they had a deliverance from the sword of the destroying angel, and afterwards from Pharaoh and the Egyptian pressures. He is therefore called 'the Lamb of God', as being fore-shadowed by the paschal lamb of the Old Testament.

All things under the law were but shadows of things to come (Heb. 10:1). Christ is the real accomplishment of all. He is our mystical, spiritual, heavenly, perfect passover. Therefore those words which are immediately spoken of the paschal lamb, and did immediately respect the passover, 'neither shall ye break a bone thereof' (Exod. 12:46 and Num. 9:12) are said to be fulfilled in Christ the antitype, as if they had been immediately pronounced of him, when they were spoken of the paschal lamb: 'For these things were done, that the scripture should be fulfilled, A bone of him shall not be broken' (John 19:36).

And indeed, if we consider all the circumstances in the institution, they seem not worthy of the wisdom of God, nor are capable of having any reason rendered for them, if they be not referred to some other mystery. And what can that be but the Redeemer of the world represented thereby? Why should so much care be in the choice and separation of a lamb? What virtue had the blood of a poor animal to secure [save] the house, and the life of the first-born against the sword of a strong and invisible angel? Was the sprinkling of the blood upon the posts a necessary mark for the angel, as though he had not understanding enough to distinguish between the houses and children of the Israelites and Egyptians? Could not God have signified his pleasure to the angel without such a mark, and given him directions for the security of his people? How can we think God should appoint so many ceremonies in it, lay such a charge upon them for the strict observation of them, if he designed it not as a prop [support] to their faith, a ground to expect a higher and spiritual deliverance by the blood of the Messiah, as well as a trial of their obedience, a memorial of their temporal deliverance, and a sign for the direction of the angel in the execution of his commission?

(2) *The believers at that time regarded it as a type of the Messiah.* 'Through faith he', that is, Moses, 'kept the passover, and the sprinkling of blood, lest he that destroyed the first-born should touch them' (Heb. 11:28). It was an illustrious testimony of Moses' faith, to rely upon the promise and goodwill of God, and keep the passover, when the blood of a lamb seems so improbable a means of preserving the Israelites from the destroying angel's sword. Yet certainly Moses' faith pierced further and looked through this shell

to the kernel, through this sign to the thing signified by it. Moses could not have esteemed the reproach of Christ (v. 26), had he not known Christ; and we cannot suppose so illustrious a prophet, that had such an estimation of Christ as to value his reproaches, did terminate [rest] his faith upon the outward action and the bare type, but pierced further to the promised Seed, as well as did Abel in his sacrifice. It is not likely that his faith stuck only in the effusion of the blood of an animal, and did not see the effusion of the blood of the Messiah, whose reproach he had been so willing to bear. It had been [would have been] too low a faith for so great a man not to regard the spiritual deliverance promised to be wrought by the bruising the heel of the Seed of the woman. Who can think Moses utterly ignorant of the design of that promise? And if not, who can think his faith should terminate in the outward sign, and that the apostle should give such encomiums [high praise] to a faith of no higher an elevation than that which respected the command of God in that present affair? Moses' faith had been [would have been] great in former commands. Why should the apostle skip over them, if he had not designed to show his [Moses'] faith in the Messiah figured in the passover?

The apostle in that chapter doth not speak of faith in God simply considered, but of faith in the Mediator or high Priest, whom he had discoursed of throughout that book. How could the ancient believers eat the same spiritual food, and drink of the same spiritual rock, which was Christ, without faith in him and respecting him as the object of faith in that rock and manna (1 Cor. 10:3, 4)? Some of the Jews acknowledge that the Messiah is to come exactly on that day in which the passover was offered, when they fled out of Egypt. And Israel was redeemed on the fifteenth day of the month Nisan, which was the day wherein Christ by his death redeemed the world. They came out of Egypt the first month, when the moon was at the full, and in the same month and the same appearance of the moon, did Christ procure our spiritual liberty by his death.

(3) *The paschal lamb was the fittest to represent Christ.*
It was a sacrifice and a feast; a sacrifice in the killing [of] it and sprinkling [of] the blood, a feast in their feeding upon it. It represents Christ as a victim satisfying God, as a feast refreshing us; he was offered to God for the expiation of our sins; he is offered to us for application to our souls. The apostle mentions one in the text, the other in the verse following, 'therefore let us keep the feast'. A lamb is both clothes and meat. Christ is clothing to us, by righteousness to cover our nakedness; and food to us, by his body and blood to satisfy our appetite. [He is] a sacrifice and a feast for us.

The truth of this proposition will appear: (1) in the resemblance between the paschal lamb and the Redeemer, and (2) in the effects or consequents of it.

1. In the resemblance between the paschal lamb and the Redeemer.

(1) *A lamb is a meek creature.* It hurts none, is hurt by all; it hangs not back when it is led to the slaughter; it cries not when it is pierced. No greater emblem of patience is to be found among irrational creatures. To this the prophet likens our Saviour when he saith: '[H]e is brought as a lamb to the slaughter, and as a sheep before her shearers is dumb, so he openeth not his mouth' (Isa. 53:7). How strange was his humility in entering into such a life! How much more

stupendous in submitting to such a death, as shameful as his life was miserable! For the Son of God to be counted the vilest of men; the Sovereign of angels to be made lower than his creatures; the Lord of heaven to become a worm of the earth; for a Creator to be spurned by his creatures is an evidence of a meekness not to be paralleled. The soldiers that spat upon him, and mocked him, met not with a reproachful expression from him. He held his peace at their clamours, offered his back to their scourges, reviled them not when he lay under the greatest violences of their rage, was patient under his sufferings, while he was despised more than any man by the people. His calmness was more stupendous than their rage, and the angels could not but more inexpressibly wonder at the patience of the sufferer, than the unmercifulness of the executioners. He was more willing to die than they were to put him to death; he suffered not by force, he courted [welcomed] the effusion [shedding] of his blood, when he knew that the hour which his Father had appointed, and man needed, was approaching. Neither the infamy [shame] of the cross, nor the sharpness of the punishment, nor the present and foreseen ingratitude of his enemies could deter him from desiring and effecting man's salvation. He went to it, not only as a duty, but [as] an honour; and was content for a while to be [the] sport of devils that he might be the spring [source] of salvation to men.

And when he was in the furnace of divine wrath, and deserted by his Father, he utters a sensible [feeling], but not a murmuring expostulation. He received our sins upon his shoulders to confer his divine benefits upon our hearts; he endured the contradiction of sinners against himself; he despised the shame, submitted to the cross; his own worldly reputation was of no value with him, so [that] he might be a sacrifice for the redemption of forlorn man. And, in the whole scene, manifested a patience greater than their cruelty. From this paschal lamb typifying the Redeemer, the Jews might have learned not to expect a Messiah wading through the world in blood and slaughter, sheathing his sword in the bodies of his enemies, and flourishing with temporal victories and prosperity; but one, meek, humble and lowly, suiting the temper of the lamb which represented him in the passover.

(2) *It was to be a lamb without blemish* (Exod. 12:5). It was to be entire in all its parts, sound without bruise or maim; and the reason why it was separated four days before the killing of it was that they might have time to understand whether it had any spot or defect in it. So is the Lamb of God. He was holy in the production of his nature, as well as in the actions of his life; though he was of Adam's substance, he was not contained in Adam's seminal virtue; he was conceived by the Holy Ghost, therefore unblemished in his conception, unspotted at his birth. From the first moment of his conception, he was filled with all supernatural grace, according to the capacity of his humanity. His union with the divine nature secured him against the sinful infirmities of our nature, and made all supernatural perfections due to him, whereby he might be fitted for all holy operations. As he was that holy thing in his birth (Luke 1:35), so he was righteous to the last moment of his life. The law of God was within his heart (signified by the tables of the law laid up in the ark, a type of his human nature), which possessed in a sovereign degree all the habits of the most accomplished righteousness that ever was in the

world. To this Peter alludes, 'a lamb without blemish and without spot' (1 Pet. 1:19), a divine idea of all virtue, who infinitely surpassed all the holiness of men or angels. The apostle multiples expressions to declare it, and all [of these are] little enough to express it: 'holy, harmless, undefiled, separate from sinners' (Heb. 7:26).

He was like us in our nature, but not in our blemishes; he had our flesh, but without the least stain of imperfection: he had the likeness of sinful flesh, but there was not any inherency [adherence] of sin in him, or adherency of it to him, in the assumption of our nature (Heb. 4:15), as the serpent upon the pole had the likeness, but not the venom of the serpent. He was not subjected to our sin, as he was to our natural infirmities; as he had the form of a servant, without the impurities of our slavery. In all the days of his flesh, he was not found guilty of one fault against God or man. It was necessary [that] he should be so. Had he been obnoxious to [liable to] sin, he had not [would not have] been able to take away the sins of the world. No impure person could have made our peace with God, because he could not have made his own peace, nor have procured quietness in his own conscience. He could not have merited for himself, much less have wrought any righteousness for others.

(3) *The lamb was to be chosen, and set apart three days and killed the fourth in the evening* (Exod. 12:6). Or between the two evenings; as it is in the Hebrew. Our Saviour was separate from men, manifested himself in the work of his prophetic office three years and upwards, before he was offered up as a sacrifice in the fourth year, after he had been solemnly inaugurated in the exercise of his office. Their keeping the

lamb in custody, and tying it at the feet of their beds, that being in view [sight] it might remind them of their servitude in Egypt. Deliverance from thence by the mighty hand of God, noted [denoted] the humiliation of Christ before his death, which is called his prison; and therefore the beginning of his exaltation is called 'He was taken from prison and from judgment' (Isa. 53:8).

As the lamb was set apart the tenth day, so some observe, that, in answer to the type, Christ did on the tenth day solemnly and in triumph enter into Jerusalem, and by the same gate through which lambs were led to sacrifice; and he was crucified that very day and time wherein the paschal lamb was to be slain, between the two evenings; that is, the declining of the sun from noon, which was the first evening, and the setting of it, which the second; for it was about the ninth hour, or three in the afternoon, the usual time wherein [at which] they killed the passover, that Christ was offered up as a complete 'sacrifice to God' (Matt. 27:46, 50). It was ordered by God to be killed in the evening, to signify the sacrifice of the Messiah in the evening of the world. He was crucified at the end of the second age of the world, the age of the law, and the beginning of the third age, that of the gospel, which is called in scripture the 'last days' (Heb. 1:2), and 'the ends of the world' (1 Cor. 10:11) which Peter alludes to, when he compares him to the paschal 'lamb without blemish ... manifest in these last times for you' (1 Pet. 1:19, 20). The death of Christ was in the first evening of the world. The sun is turned; the world shall not last so long after the coming of Christ, as it did before. The state of the world is far declined, and the consummation of all things is not far off, since more than sixteen hundred years are past since the first evening began.

(4) *The lamb was to be roasted with fire whole, not sodden* [boiled] (Exod. 12:8, 9). To put them in mind of the hardship they endured in the brick-kilns of Egypt, and as a type of the scorching sufferings of the Redeemer, whose 'strength is dried up like a potsherd and my tongue cleaveth to my jaws' (Ps. 22:15), probably alluding to this roasting of the paschal lamb. He bore the wrath of that God who is a consuming fire, without any water, any mitigation or comfort in his torments. It may note also the gradual rising of the suffering of Christ. As his exaltation was not all at one time, but by degrees, so were his sufferings, by outward wounds, cutting reproaches and inward agonies. The pains of the body were inexpressible in regard of the nervousness, and therefore sensibility [sensitivity], of those parts, his hands and feet, which were pierced upon the cross. The consideration of those millions of sins laid upon him could not but be an inexpressible grief to the pure nature of Christ, had there been nothing of the wrath of God mixed with it.

But his bodily death and grief was not all. The wrath of God dreadfully flamed out against his soul. There [i.e. in his soul] was the principal seat of the sufferings of Christ, because the soul is the principal seat of that sin for which he suffered. What should have been inflicted upon us, was inflicted upon him. But we had not only merited the death of the body, but a death joined with the curse of God tormenting the soul. He tasted death, the death which the devil had the power of, that 'fear of death' (Heb. 2:9, 14, 15), which is the weight of that eternal death due to sin. How sharp must that be, which had the bitterness of a thousand deaths, for those millions of sins which Christ bore in his body, every one of which had deserved an entire death from the hand of God! How grievous was that death, since he that was more courageous than all the martyrs, sweat [sweated] drops of blood at the approach of the cross; and when he was upon it, uttered that terrible complaint, 'My God! my God! why hast thou forsaken me?', words which never came out of the mouth of any of the martyrs in the strength of their torments. So that the sufferings of Christ were of that [such] weight, that a mere creature would have sunk under them – not only the holiest man, but the highest angel.

(5) *Not a bone of the paschal lamb was broken* (Exod. 12:46). Which, according to the opinion of some, signified that kind of death to which the breaking of the bones belonged, and that was crucifixion. For it was the custom to break the bones of malefactors, that their punishment might be shortened. This was fulfilled in our Saviour (John 19:36). Death had not a full power over him. He was not broken to pieces by the greatness of his sufferings, but surmounted his enemies upon the cross, and was reserved entire for a resurrection.

There may be other resemblances noted. As the lamb was to be a male, which implies the perfection and strength of the sacrifice, not above a year old, the sufferings of Christ were in the prime of his age.

2. There is a resemblance in the effects or consequences of the passover.

(1) *The diverting [of] the destroying angel by the sprinkling of the blood upon the posts, to be a mark to the angel, to spare the first-born of such houses, was the main end expressed in the institution* (Exod. 12:12, 13). Their preservation could not be merited by the blood of an animal. It had a higher

cause, the blood of Christ, which was represented by it; to which purpose the observation [comment] of Chrysostom[1] is remarkable. As the statues of kings, though they are inanimate [lifeless] things, yet are sanctuaries to preserve those that fly [flee] to them, not because they are statues, but because they represent the prince; so the blood of the Lamb preserved the families, not because it was blood, but because it represented the blood of the Messiah. This blood quenches that fire of wrath we had merited, turns away that vengeance which would else consume us. By virtue of this sacrifice, we pass 'from death unto life' (John 5:24). When God shall judge the world, he will pass over those whom he sees sprinkled with the blood of his Well-beloved, and turn from them the edge of that consuming sword, which shall strike through the hearts of those that are without this blood of sprinkling. It is only under the warrant of this blood that we can be safe. The Redeemer's blood shed for us, and sprinkled on us, preserves our souls to eternal life. As the destroying sword did not touch the Israelites, so condemning wrath shall not strike those that are under the protection of the blood. Death shall have no power over them. The blood of the paschal lamb wrought [brought about] a temporal deliverance, and this blood a spiritual and eternal one.

(2) *Upon this succeeded [followed] that liberty [deliverance] which God had designed for them* (Exod. 12:31). As it secured them from death, so it was the earnest [foretaste] of their deliverance, and broke the chains of their slavery. The death of Christ is the foundation of the full deliverance of his people, and the earnest [foretaste] of the fruition [enjoyment] of the

---

1   One of the Early Church Fathers (c. 344-407).

purchased and promised inheritance. This was the conquest of Pharaoh, upon which soon after followed his destruction. Pharaoh's heart was not bent [subdued] till the celebration of this passover. That which succeeded it laid him more flat than all the former plagues whereby [under which] he had smarted. The promises concerning the Messiah, and the sacrifices which were types of him, terrified the devil, Pharaoh's antitype; but only the blood of Christ shed, conquers him, and pulls captives from his chains.

The Israelites' slavery ended, when their sacrifices were finished; the efficacy of this Divine Passover delivers men from a spiritual captivity, under the yoke of sin, and the irons of Satan, and instates them in the liberty of the children of God, whereby they become a holy nation, a royal priesthood, a free and peculiar people. This strikes off the shackles, works an escape from the pressures of spiritual enemies, changes a deplorable captivity into a glorious liberty, and reduces Satan to so impotent a condition that all his strength, and all his stratagems, cannot render him master of that soul that is once freed from his chains. As after this passover, the Egyptian strength was so scattered, that they were as ready to force that people to their liberty, as before they were desirous to detain them their slaves, and were never able to reduce [bring them back] them to their former chains.

(3) *After this passover they do not only enjoy their liberty, but begin their march to Canaan, the promised and delightful land.* They then turn their backs upon Egypt, and their faces towards Canaan; and, after a pilgrimage in the desert, they enter into the land flowing with milk and honey. So, by the merit of the sacrifice of Christ, the true Israelite turns his face from earth to heaven, from a world that lies

in wickedness, to an inheritance of the saints in light, and travels towards [the heavenly] Canaan, whither he shall be sure to enter after he hath finished his pilgrimage, to feed upon the milk and honey, the glory and happiness proper to that state. Then shall all the ends [aims] of this passover be fulfilled and completed 'in the kingdom of God' (Luke 22:16), and the soul remain for ever in a glorious state beyond the reach of its former tyrants, free from all fear of slavery, for ever rejoicing in the happy accomplishment of the promises of God. In short, as after the celebration of this passover in Egypt, all the promises of God began to take place, and pass into performance; so by the death of Christ, the true passover, all the promises were made yea and amen, in him, and began to be made good to every believer.

Practical Applications

1. Of [For] information. Is Christ called our passover? Then,

(1) *The study of the Old Testament is advantageous [beneficial].* The apostle here writes to the Corinthians, among whom were not only Hellenites, but Gentiles, who could not understand the nature and ends of the passover without the knowledge of the Old Testament; by this they are implicitly directed to the study of it. The Old Testament verifies the New, and the New illustrates the Old. The Old shows the promises of God, and the New the performance. What was predicted in the Old is fulfilled in the New. By comparing both together, the wisdom of God in his conduct is cleared, and the truth of God in his word confirmed. The Old Testament delivers the types, the New interprets them. The Old presents them like money in a bag; the New spreads them, and discovers the value of the coin. The Israelites in

the Old felt the weight of the ceremonies, believers in the New enjoy the riches of them.

(2) *Upon what a slender thread doth the doctrine of transubstantiation[2] hang!* Christ is here called the passover; was the paschal lamb therefore substantially the body of Christ? Were those lambs that were slain in Egypt, or at any other time in the celebration of this ordinance, transubstantiated into Christ? Yet Christ is as absolutely here called the passover, and in other places, the lamb, as the bread in the sacrament is called his body, or the wine his blood. Christ is said to be the rock, of which the Israelites drank (1 Cor. 10:4). Was the rock or the water that flowed from it transubstantiated into Christ? But in scripture the name proper to the thing represented is given to that which represents it. The lamb is called the passover because it is a memorial of the angel's passing over the Israelites' families, and not only called so at the first institution, but above fifteen hundred years after that miraculous mercy. So the bread and wine are called the body and blood of Christ, because they are memorials and signs of his body and blood. If the church of the Jews spake figuratively in the case of the passover, what difficulty is it, that Christ should call the memorials of his body and blood by the name of the things they signified?

(3) *It gives us a probable reason for the change of the sabbath from the seventh day to the first.* That it is changed, is evident by apostolical example (see Lightfoot's[3] *Gleanings*

---

2   The Roman Catholic Theory that in the Lord's Supper, the bread is literally changed into the Body of Christ and the wine into his blood.

3   John Lightfoot (1602 -1675), an English biblical scholar who had profound knowledge of the Old Testament.

on Exodus 12:2). It is probable that from the creation the year began in September, the autumnal equinox, the fruits being on the trees at the creation; but now God orders the beginning of the year from the time of the first passover, and the consequences following upon it, their deliverance from Egypt, which was in March [at] the vernal [spring] equinox: 'This month shall be unto you the beginning of months: it shall be the first month of the year to you' (Exod. 12:2). Had the year began from March at the beginning, it had not been [would not have been] so proper to command them to begin it from that month, which they had always observed before as the beginning of the year. The Israelites had been as it were 'buried' in Egypt, and this, being the month of their 'resurrection', should be the first month of the year. This change of the beginning of the year gives us a probable reason for the change of the sabbath. If the beginning of the year were changed upon the account of the type, a day might well be changed upon the account of the antitype. If this in the figure were counted greater than creation, that the month of the world's creation must give place to it, the substance of this figure appearing might well be the cause of the change of a day; and the seventh day of the creation give place to the first day of the perfection of redemption.[4]

(4) *The ancient Jews were under a covenant of grace.* Christ was the end, the spirit, the life of their sacrifices. The passover, rock, sacrifices, manna, were the swaddling-bands wherein he was wrapt. They ate of the same spiritual meat, drank of the same spiritual drink: the rock which followed them,

---

4   To the modern reader the above sounds obscure. We believe, however, that God changed the weekly Sabbath from the last day to the first day of the week to honour Christ's resurrection on that day. Ed.

cherished them and watered them, was Christ (1 Cor. 10:3, 4). Christ to come was set forth to them as an object of faith. Christ was the rock, the passover sacramentally. Their sacraments and ours were the same in effect, though diverse [different] in signs [elements]. Hence their sacraments [circumcision and the passover] are attributed to us spiritually: ours in the same manner to them, baptism and the Lord's Supper (1 Cor. 10:2, 3). They indeed had Christ, as it were, in his infancy; we in his ripe and full age. They had him under the obscure veil of lambs, bullocks, goats; we have him in his person. They had the sun under a cloud; we [have] the sun at noon-day in its glory.

2. Comfort

(1) *In the security Christ procures.* The destroying angel was not to enter into any sprinkled house. No passage [access] was afforded to him. The wrath of God, or the malice of the devil, can have no power over them that are sprinkled with the blood of Christ.

(2) *In the efficacy.* The blood of the lamb was but a sign of that deliverance of the Israelites, but could not purge their defiled consciences. But the blood of our Lamb has merited our salvation, it can cleanse our consciences from dead and condemning works, to serve the living God, and rejoice in him, who without this sprinkling will be to us a consuming fire. As the passover was killed, that it might be their food as well as their security; so was Christ crucified that he might be our atonement and our nourishment, our shield and our food, to make us partakers of his benefits by a spiritual application, and a close incorporation of us with himself.

This comfort is the greater, in that the tyrant we are delivered from is more dreadful than Pharaoh, whose design [intention] is not only, like his, to afflict our bodies, but to plunge our souls and bodies into the same hell with [as] himself.

It is from the wrath of God that our passover hath delivered us. And what is the anger of Pharaoh to the fury of an offended Deity [God], kindled against us by our multiplied transgressions?

It is true, deliverance is yet but [now only just] begun; it is not yet perfect. Miseries, and spiritual contests are to be expected. Pharaoh will pursue, but shall not overtake; the sea shall ruin the Egyptians, but secure the Israelites; death shall not swallow up those who are sprinkled with this holy blood.

Consider also, if God were so punctual to [exact in keeping] his word in so light [slight] an instance as the blood of the lamb, he will be as steadfast to it in so great an instance as the blood of his Son beheld [when he sees it] cleaving to [sprinkled on] the soul.

3. Exhortation

(1) *Thankfully remember this passover.* A redemption from divine wrath, a spiritual life and liberty, the fruits and purchase of this Lamb, are incomparably beyond the temporal deliverance conferred upon the Jews. The giving thanks was a duty annexed to the eating of the paschal lamb, wherein [in which] they blessed God for the mercy showed to their fathers in bringing them out of Egypt. How infinitely more precious is the blood of the Son of God than the blood of a silly [dumb] animal! How highly doth the benefit of the one surmount the immediate fruit of the other! And is it

not fit our praises should surpass those of the Jews for the old passover?

Remember it with bitterness. The Israelites ate the passover with bitter herbs. Shall we be without it, when we consider the cause of our slavery, and the means of our deliverance? A bitterness of soul[5] will make the taste of the benefit of Christ more delicious.

(2) *Inquire whether he be our passover.* He is a passover, but is he a lamb eaten by us, owned by us? He is ours by the gift of God, but is he ours by the acceptation [acceptance] of our souls? It is the most useful, most necessary inquiry we can make. All the comfort of possessions in the world consists in the word 'mine', 'ours', and the use [of them] as ours. All the comfort of spiritual mercy consists in property [ownership], possession and fruition [enjoyment]. If he be our Lamb, we must be like him, we must learn of him. As he is the cause of our expiation, [so] he must be the copy of our imitation, '[L]earn of me; for I am meek and lowly in heart: and ye shall find rest unto your souls' (Matt. 11:29). No rest without a sense of sin, and humiliation for it. This Lamb is ours in the liberty, life, glory and rest he has purchased, when we are like him and when we learn of him.

(3) *Have faith in the blood of Christ.* The killing [of] the lamb signified the death of Christ; the sprinkling [of] the blood signified the application of it by faith. It was not the blood contained in the veins of the lamb, or shed upon the ground, that was the mark of deliverance, but sprinkled upon the posts; nor is it the blood of Christ circulating in

---

5 Charnock means by this that Christians should stir themselves up to repentance. Ed.

his body, or shed upon the cross, which solely delivers us, but as applied by faith to the heart. The one was sprinkled upon every house which desired safety, and the other upon every soul that desires happiness.

Satan will have an undoubted right over all that are without the token of this blood, as the destroying angel had over every house that was not sprinkled with the blood of the passover.

This was the sanctuary of the Israelites: the want of it, the death of the Egyptian first-born, from the prince to the peasant, from him that sat upon the throne to him that was in the dungeon (Exod. 12:29). Without this blood of sprinkling, neither prince nor beggar can possibly escape. The one's grandeur cannot privilege [entitle], nor the other's misery procure pity.

The blood was to be taken and put upon the posts. This condition was requisite. To have a part in the great passover of our Lord, the condition is to sprinkle our hearts by faith with his blood (1 Pet. 1:2). Had an Israelite's family neglected this, it had [would have] felt the edge of the angel's sword; the lamb had not [would not have] availed him, not by a defect of the sacrifice, but by their own negligence or contempt of the condition. Or had they used any other mark [i.e. on the posts of their door], they had not [would not have] diverted the stroke. No work, no blood, but the blood and sufferings of the Redeemer can take away the sin of the world. Without it every man in the world lies in the sin of his nature under the wrath of God. If any thing else in the world had a virtue for it [power in it], it could not prevail [avail], unless God would accept it, because he did not appoint it. This only is designed to be our passover. Where else can we find any remedy against the stings of our consciences, any ease under the weight of our sins, any consolation against divine wrath?

(4) *Let us leave the service of sin.* The Israelites after this passover did no more work at the brick-kilns of Egypt; they ceased to be Pharaoh's slaves, and began to be the Lord's freemen. God intended no more to turn them to their former labour; he would have them eat their passover with their loins girt in the habit [dress] of travellers. We must be in a readiness to leave the confines of Egypt, all commerce with, and service of sin and Satan, and have our faces set towards Canaan, our steps directed to observe his commands for our rule, to attain his promises for our comfort, and go forward rejoicing in his goodness, celebrating his name, offering our souls and bodies to him. This is a reasonable service to Christ our passover.

Part 2: Christ is a Sacrifice

The word 'sacrifice' properly signifies to kill as a sacrifice. Some dispute whether the paschal lamb was a sacrifice, because in a sacrifice something was offered to God either in whole or in part; but the paschal lamb was not offered to God, but eaten by the people; it was killed, to the end that the blood should be sprinkled upon the posts of the doors, and therefore it is rather a sacrament than a sacrifice. Again, the Jews did not sacrifice out of the temple, and therefore in their captivities they did not sacrifice but both then and now they celebrate the passover. Others again think it a sacrifice, because the sprinkling of the blood upon the posts was in a manner an offering [of] it to God to turn away his wrath: 'Thou shalt not offer the blood of my sacrifice with leaven; neither shall the sacrifice of the feast of the passover be left unto the morning' (Exod. 34:25); and a means of reconciliation to him: 'Thou shalt therefore sacrifice the passover unto the LORD' (Deut. 16:2). But whether properly a sacrifice or not, yet it signified the propitiating blood of Christ, the future grand sacrifice by virtue of which we have our deliverance. The apostle might here allude to the passover and other sacrifices, all which did prefigure the spiritual redemption by the Messiah. A sacrifice is defined to be, a religious oblation of something consecrated and dedicated to God by the ministry of a priest according to God's institution, to be offered for a testimony of the worship of God and an external symbol.

I shall lay down some propositions [leading ideas] for the illustrating [of] this doctrine.

Sacrifices were instituted as types of Christ
(1) They were instituted by God. No satisfactory reason can be rendered of [for] the custom of sacrificing derived from the first age of the world, practised by all nations, till the appearance of the gospel abolished it in those places where it shone. It could not be a dictate of the law of nature inscribed in all men's hearts, for then they would have been of force still. Christianity does not extinguish any beam of natural light, but adds a clearness to it; it abolishes only what was corrupt or only ceremonial. Though natural light could not invent them, yet it made them entertainable by all, while they were stung with the conscience [consciousness] of sin and expectations of vengeance. Men might know that they were unlike what they were in their creation; they found their light darkened, their beauty defaced, and might suppose that a God of infinite goodness did not send them forth in such a shape out of his mint; this deformity must [have] come upon them for some provocation and by the means of their own sin. They also found the marks of God's

anger upon them, saw and felt his thundering judgments in the world, they had a notion of the vindictive [retributive] justice of God, they had frequent manifestations of it upon themselves and others. This the apostle affirms generally of the heathens, 'Who knowing the judgment of God, that they which commit such things are worthy of death' (Rom. 1:32). They had a sentiment of God and revenging justice in their consciences, that it did not become [befit] the holiness and righteousness of the divine nature to let their rebellions remain unpunished. The apostle speaks not there of any supernatural revelation, but [of] the natural manifestation by the creatures, whereby God's justice was discovered as well as his eternal power and Godhead.

Upon this account sacrifices were practised among them, as seeming to them congruous means for the expiation of sin and to put a stop to the wrath of God, either feared by them or already kindled among them. For by this action they confessed their desert of death for their crimes, acknowledged God's sovereignty and right over all they had, and owned his mercy in accepting in their stead the life of an irrational [non-rational] animal. For when men are sensible [aware] of the anger of God, the next thought in order is how to escape it.

When men see a magistrate suffer [allow] murders and violences in a nation to go unpunished, they generally have a horror of it, and expect some judgment of God, till an expiation be made by the death of the offender. And could they reasonably think God to be void of that virtue of justice, which is commendable over all the world by the light of nature, when those perfections of human nature, left in the midst of corruption, are but as little sparks to those which are infinite in God? They were at first instituted by

God; though we have not the institution of them in express words, yet we have the practice in Abel (Gen. 4:4), afterwards in Noah, 'Noah ... offered burnt offerings on the altar' (Gen. 8:20). And since the apostle speaks of Abel's offering a sacrifice in faith (Heb. 11:4), it must be God's command; for no act of worship of a human invention can please God. The demand might be made, '[W]ho hath required this at your hand' (Isa. 1:12)? It had not been [would not have been] formally good, unless offered in faith; nor had it been a fit ground or medium of faith, without a divine stamp upon it. If the foundation [i.e. reason for offering it] were not divine, the act could not be acceptable.

(2) No other reason can be rendered of [for] the institution of them, but as typical of the great sacrifice of the Redeemer. The scripture gives us the only account of this; all nations in the world without the scripture are in the dark as to the design of those sacrifices, though they practised them conformably to the sentiments of their consciences. The institution of them from the beginning of the world cannot reasonably be concluded to be for any other end than to prefigure some sufficient sacrifice, able to appease the wrath of God and pacify the consciences of men, and to instruct men in what was to be brought upon the stage in time, in the exhibition of the person of the Redeemer.

In the state of innocence we find no mention of them, nor could they have had any place, had man continued in his created rectitude [uprightness] and integrity. The covenant of works, which then was the rule and ground of man's standing, required not faith in a Redeemer, and therefore implied no such act as sacrificing. Man then had no relation to God but as a creature; and, persisting in obedience, could not by the righteous law of God be subject to death, and therefore no other subjected to death for him; for to have any one to die for us implies that we had merited death ourselves. It cannot enter into the reason of man to imagine what use they could be for in that state. Death was not due to the righteousness of man's nature, but to his corruption. Adam stood upon his own foundation [i.e. righteousness], and was the foundation of all his posterity, and no person was substituted in his room. What could sacrifices then represent? Whereof could they be typical? Could they be for the confession of sin? There was none to confess. Could they be to represent a death deserved? There was no crime committed whereby to merit it. Could it be to typify Christ to come? There was no revelation of him till after the fall (Gen. 3:15). And supposing, as some do, that Christ should have been incarnate had man persisted in his first integrity; yet none suppose Christ should have been crucified in that nature, without the entrance of sin. What end could be supposed of shedding his blood? For satisfaction of justice? Justice was not provoked [offended]. For example [i.e. to set him a good example]? Man perfect in all virtue needed none; besides, he was not capable of the exercise of suffering virtues, who was not capable of suffering in that state. They were appointed therefore after the fall, as representations of this sacrifice so necessary for the expiation of sin.

Some conclude, with probability, that they were put in practice immediately after making the promise of the Seed of the woman, though there could be no express scripture for it; yet from Genesis 3:21, 'God make[s] coats of skins', which probably were the skins of slain beasts, very likely consumed by fire from heaven; as the Jews say Abel's sacrifice was, which was a token of God's acceptation [acceptance] of it. This was probably done for the confirmation of the truth of the promise, the clearer representing the design of it to them, by substituting another in the room of the offender, and comforting them thereby, since 'without shedding of blood is no remission' (Heb. 9:22). And of those sacrifices the skins were appointed to be the garments of the first man and woman, to put them in mind of their apostasy and the way of their recovery, by the righteousness of another wherein they were to stand before God.

But howsoever it be, we cannot suppose Abel to be the first that offered sacrifice, and that one hundred and twenty-nine years should run without the offering of any. It is likely Abel was slain in that year, because Seth was born in the one hundred and thirtieth year of Adam's age (Gen. 5:3). Indeed, sacrifices, as they looked backward, could be no other than a transcript of the agreement between the Father and the Son, of the one's paying and the other's accepting the price of blood for the redemption of man; and as they looked forward, a type of the real performance of the sufferings on the one part and the acceptance of them on the other part, when the fullness of time should come wherein they were actually to be undergone. This tradition of sacrifices was handed down to all nations of the world, but the knowledge of the end [purpose] of them was lost. Yet in an exercise of reason they might rise to a consideration that this: low blood [blood of beasts] could not be a compensation for sin, as not being proportioned to the dignity of him with whom they had to do. But as to the true end of them, the representation of a higher sacrifice, they were not able to discern it by all the reason in the world, after they had lost the revelation of it. By the way [Incidentally], this adds a credit to the scripture, since it gives us an account of the reason of that which was practised by all nations, which they could not without revelation render any tolerable reason for. The scripture makes it plain. God would have a representation of that which the Redeemer was to offer in the fullness of time for the abolition of sin. As men always need a satisfaction of the justice of God, so God would have it that in all their worship there should be a mark of this necessity, and some presage [foreshadowing] that one day there should be a sacrifice eternally efficacious, the reality of which was represented by this figure [symbol, i.e. blood sacrifice].

3. Christ did really answer to these types.

They were all Christ in a cloud, the substance did answer to the shadows, and he was used in such a manner as the figures of him were. Christ was a victim put in the place of the sinner to appease the anger of God; and as sins were laid upon the head of the sacrifice, so God put 'on him the iniquity of us all' (Isa. 53:6). In regard of this typicalness of the legal administration, Christ is often called a lamb, and the 'Lamb of God' (John 1:29), and a Lamb slain from the foundation of the world, not only in the decree, but in the type of him, the first sacrifice mentioned in the scripture which was a firstling of the flock (Gen. 4:2, 4), Abel being the keeper of sheep. To those figures of him he seems to refer in his last speech upon the cross (John 19:30), 'It is finished'. The whole design of the daily and extraordinary sacrifices was completed, the demerit of sin and severity of divine justice were manifested, and the truth of God, as well as his love, made glorious therein; upon which followed the rending of the veil, and the setting [of] heaven open for the entrance of all that believed in him to approach to God upon the account of this sacrifice.

The sacrifices thus instituted were of themselves insufficient, and could not expiate sin; they must therefore receive their accomplishment in some other.

Being but shadows by their institution, they could make nothing perfect (Heb. 10:1, 11, where [in this chapter], and in the following verses, the apostle lays the glory of the legal sacrifices in the dust), nor really atone, though they typically did. They did but evidence the guilt of sin and misery of men, whence the law is called a minister of death.

(1) *It was not consistent with the honour of God to be contented with the blood of a beast for the expiation of sin.* How could there be in it a discovery of the severity of his justice, the purity of his holiness, or the grandeurs of his grace? How would he have been known in his infinite hatred of sin, if he had accepted the blood of an abject animal as an atonement for the sin of a spiritual soul? Was it becoming [consistent with] the majesty of God, who had denounced a curse in the law upon the transgressors of it, and published it with so terrible a solemnity as thunders, lightnings and earthquakes which made it pass under the title of a 'fiery law' (Deut. 33:2) in regard of the severe menaces against the transgressor, to make so light of it to accept of the mangling a few beasts in the place of the offender against it? Should he appear on Mount Sinai with ten thousand of his angels in the giving of it, to let all the threatenings of it vanish into smoke? Was it likely [that] all those curses should be poured out upon a few irrational and innocent creatures who had never broken that law? Can it be imagined, that after so terrible a proclamation, he should acquiesce in so light a compensation as the death of a poor beast? No man can reasonably have such despicable thoughts of the majesty, justice and holiness of God or the vileness of sin

and greatness of its provocation, as to imagine that the one could be contented or the other expiated by the blood of a lamb or bullock. Our own consciences will tell us that if God will have a sacrifice, it must be proportioned to the majesty of him whom we have offended and the greatness of the crime we have committed.

(2) *They have no proportion to the sin of man.* The sin of a rational creature is too foul to be expiated by the blood of an irrational creature; nor could the blood of a human body, though the first-born, the strength and delight of man (Micah 6:7) much less of a beast, bear any proportion to the sin of the soul: 'it is not possible that the blood of bulls and of goats should take away sins' (Heb. 10:4). The butchery of so poor a creature cannot be any compensation for that which is a disparagement of the Creator of the world. What alliance was there between the nature of a beast and that of a man? An inferior nature can never atone for the sin of a nature superior to it. There is indeed in the groans of those dying creatures some demonstration of God's wrath, but no bringing in an everlasting righteousness nor any vindication of the honour of the law.

(3) *The reiteration of them shows their insufficiency.* Had the wrath of God been appeased by them, why should the fire burn perpetually upon the altar? Why should it be fed perpetually with the carcases of beasts? As often as they were offered, a conscience of sin was excited in the presenter of them, iniquity was called to remembrance (Heb. 10:2, 3). The whole scene of that administration loudly published that the wrath against sin was not appeased, the guilt of the soul not wiped off. If a man had presented a sacrifice for his sin one day and fallen into the same or another before night,

he must have repeated [required to repeat] his sacrifice for a new expiation. [But] had there been ability in them to perform so great a thing, there had not been [would not have been] a repetition. They were rather a commemoration of sin, and confession of it, than expiations of any. [They were] rather accusers than atoners.

(4) *God had often spoken slightly [slightingly] of them.* He resembles them to the cutting off a dog's neck, when done with an unholy heart (Isa. 66:3). [Even] while the temple stood [was still standing], he struck their fingers off[6] from hanging [trusting on them as if automatic] upon them (Isa. 1:11-13). Indeed he would not reprove them for their offerings (Ps. 50:8); but he would not have them place their justification in them. He professes [that] he had no delight in them (Ps. 40:6). If all sacrifices of the law were not of such value as love to him and fear of him, they could not expiate; and if that which was more excellent than those were too weak to effect it, an utter inability must remain in the other. He does frequently predict the abolition of them, and has destroyed the temple to which he had affixed them, which remains in desolation without a sacrifice to this day.

Besides, he never provided a typical remedy for all sins in them; some transgressors were to be cut off without a sacrifice for them, according to the judicial law, the rule of the government of that people; upon which account David argues that God did not delight in them: '[T]hou desirest not sacrifice ... thou delightest not in burnt offering' (Ps. 51:16), because he had provided no sacrifices for those sins David at that time was guilty of. Whereupon

---

6   By this unusual expression Charnock evidently means that God discouraged them. Ed.

he desires in verse 18 that God would do good to Sion in his good pleasure; bring forth that Redeemer out of Sion which he had promised, whose sacrifice being a sacrifice of righteousness should be infinitely delightful to him.

Since therefore it is unbecoming [unsuitable for] the majesty of God to be satisfied with the blood of a calf or goat, since it bears no proportion to the sin of man, since he never intended those institutions to be perpetual, since the threatenings of the law must, if God be a God of truth, have their accomplishment either in the person offending or in some undertaker for him capable of bearing them in his stead; there must be some other sacrifice suited to the majesty of God, able to make an expiation proportionable to the sin of man, a sacrifice able to remove the guilt, and pacify the conscience; a rest for God and a security for the creature. The natural order of things requires, and the whole design of those legal institutions declares, that as he that keeps the law should have a reward from the goodness of God, so he that breaks it should endure a punishment from the justice of God. And every man being [since every man is] a breaker of the [Moral] law must either sink under the menaces of it or present a sufficient sacrifice to God to avert his [God's] wrath. [Such a man must offer] a precious blood that may quench the flames of his anger, so that God may say to the sinner, 'I have found, and accepted, a ransom for thee'. And what is said of this may be said of all our duties and performances, the staves [staff, i.e. basis of confidence] upon which men naturally lean for acceptation [acceptance] of their persons. They [religious services] can no more be acceptable in themselves to God, or remedies for man, than the legal sacrifices which had no merit in themselves but represented that which was grateful [pleasing] to God and meritorious for the creature; and whatsoever virtue and efficacy they had was not of themselves, but from that which they foreshadowed.

Such a sacrifice therefore is necessary for a sinful creature.
No creature can be such a sacrifice; as the apostle argues, '[I]f righteousness come by the law, then Christ is dead in vain' (Gal. 2:21). Upon the same account, it may be concluded that if expiation could be made by a creature for himself, in vain did God send his Son to be a propitiation for sin. Had man himself been sufficient for it, God's sending his Son had [would have] rather appeared an act of cruelty to Christ, than of mercy to us. Who could think God should expose the delight of his soul to our infirmities and a shameful death, if a sufficient sacrifice could have been found elsewhere? Besides, the wrath of God being so terrible that the human nature of Christ trembled at it, how is any creature ever able to bear the horror of it and stand as a sacrifice under the weighty strokes of that justice?

(1) *What is sacrifice for sin must be pure and sinless.* God will not accept a defiled offering. He that provokes him by his own offence is not capable of appeasing him for his own or other's. The least blemish in a typical lamb rendered it unfit for the altar. God is infinitely pure, who is offended; the law is exactly holy, which is broken. A compensation cannot be made to a holy God and a righteous law by the criminal, without enduring an infinite penalty, which, since it cannot be infinite, it must be perpetual [eternal]. As he would be always suffering, so he would be always sinning, and wrath can never be appeased by that which provokes it at the same time [as] it endeavours to pacify it. What is sinful can never be capable of pleasing an [i.e. God's] infinite

holiness. If a man had but one sin and thought to expiate that by any thing he could do, he would still need another sacrifice to expiate the sin of the former, and so would be always satisfying and always sinning, since there is 'not a just man ... that doeth good, and sinneth not' (Eccles. 7:20) in the doing of it. He could not possibly find any thing in himself, or in any corrupted creature, where he might rest his foot [i.e. hope of acceptance with God] with any happiness and security. Where any sin is, though it is one, there can be no merit. Whatsoever is done after all our strength is gone, is done by the grace of God; in that case God deserves service of us, but we deserve no acceptation [acceptance] from him. Since therefore we are not [cap-] able, since our fall, of doing one good work [and] we are not able to offer one acceptable sacrifice; how can man then satisfy for himself. A man who owes a shilling cannot repay it by borrowing two. He is so far from paying his debts, that he increase them!

(2) *An infinite sacrifice is necessary for a sin [which is] in some respects infinite; for every sin intrencheth [intrudes] upon the honour of an infinite God.* An infinite sacrifice is due for an infinite offence. God is infinite in his glory, which is impaired [by man's sin]; infinite in his sovereignty, which is degraded. The sacrifice must be of as great a dignity as the offence was of malignity. It must be fully proportioned to the sin of man and the majesty of God. What man, indeed, for that matter, what creature is capable of such a proportion? The condition of his nature is too low and the limits of his dignity too strait [limited], to correspond with such an effect. The 'drop of a bucket, and ... the small dust of the balance', are of too vile a nature to be a satisfactory sacrifice to God. All men are no more (Isa. 40:15-17). Indeed man is 'less than nothing, and vanity'. And therefore all men in the

world put together would be so far from redeeming themselves by a sufficient sacrifice, that both they themselves and also their sacrifice would be worse than nothing and vanity and would be overwhelmed under the punishment due to their offence. Finite bears no proportion to infinite. Therefore a finite sacrifice carries no equivalent compensation in it for an infinite wrong. So that neither length of time nor strength of nature can ever make a recompense for that offence which increaseth in proportion according to the dignity of the person against whom it is committed.

If every hair of our head were a soul, and every soul a sacrifice, all would be too poor an amends for that glorious God wronged by us, though it had been but by one [single] act of rebellion. For man cannot do any act of that value in the nature of satisfaction, as one act of sin is injurious in the nature of wrong. Upon the same account of finiteness, no angel could be a proportionable [proportionate] sacrifice to the justice of God for the sin of man. For though the excellence of the angelic far transcends the nature of man, yet it cannot equal the dignity of God. They are creatures and an inconceivable distance is perpetually between creatures and the Creator. Therefore saith Job, '[H]e put no trust in his servants; and his angels he charged with folly' (Job 4:18). All the excellency of the angelic nature is despicable compared with God. And if God did not secure them, they would fall; if God did not preserve light in them, they would be darkness [sinful] as well as we [are]. If they could not [make amends] because they are [mere] creatures, man could not because he was a sinful creature. '[T]housands of rams, or with ten thousands of rivers of oil' would have borne far less proportion to the Creator of them, or to sins against him (Micah 6:6, 7).

(3) *It is necessary too in regard of the justice of God, which is an immutable and infinite perfection of the divine essence.* God is so infinitely holy that it is impossible for him not to hate the least sin. He is infinite in his justice and cannot let any sin go unpunished since he hath declared by his law that 'cursed is everyone that continueth not in all things which are written in the book of the law to do them' (Gal. 3:10) and that it was irrevocably past that 'in the day that thou eatest' of the forbidden fruit, he should 'surely die' (Gen. 2:17). As the perfection of his nature requires that he should have for sin an implacable aversion; so the same perfection requires that [his own] justice be not appeased without punishment. Since God therefore would have a sacrifice for sin, to have one disproportioned to his infinite dignity and justice had been [would have] the same as to have [had] none at all. An infinite sacrifice cannot be offered but by an infinite person. It was necessary therefore that one of the persons of the Trinity should be this sacrifice. And it was most congruous to [consistent with] the wisdom of God, for several reasons, that it should be the second Person of the Trinity, Jesus Christ.

This sacrifice is necessary at least in point of becomingness [fitness], as God is the author of all things, and placed them in a rectitude from which they departed by their own folly and sullied [defiled] that glory [which] they were created to manifest. It became [befitted] him to bring things into order again by such a method as should manifest his hatred of that disorder [which] sin had introduced into the world. In this way God would show how strict a guardian he would be of the eternal order of things and of those sacred laws whereby he governs the world: 'It became him, for whom are all things, and by whom are all things, in bringing many sons unto glory, to make the captain of their salvation perfect through sufferings' (Heb. 2:10). As God had made all things for his glory, so it was fit that his Son, becoming the head of the world, should be put in such a posture [condition] as to show forth the glory of God in the most illustrious manner. Now in the sufferings of Christ, the justice of God flames more bright[-ly] than it could in any creature and shows itself inflexible [unmovably stern] against sin. The treasures of his grace are wider opened than could be in any other act. And his wisdom sparkles [shines] more gloriously in bringing men to glory by punishment. And since he made all things, and that for himself, it became him, after the apostasy of man and the defacing the creation, to restore things in such a way as might conduce most to his own glory and the happiness of the creature.

Christ only was fit to be this sacrifice.
Whatsoever any creature could have done had been [would have] a debt of duty and that could not have made a compensation for a debt of rebellion. Whatsoever a mere creature could do was by the gift of God and therefore could not merit any thing at the hand of God. Whatsoever is meritorious must be our own as well as that which is not due. Besides, from any other hand God would have received less than the offence merited; at the best it would have been but a feigned [pretended] and partial satisfaction which had not been [would not have been] congruous to [consistent with] the wisdom and justice of God, since he determined it necessary to have a sacrifice.

But Christ in his divine nature was 'equal with God' (Phil. 2:6) and therefore in his person [he] was answerable to the dignity of the person offended; and as he was in the form of a servant and innocent, he offered that which was not due from himself, and upon his own account, to God. For though as a creature he was bound to the obedience of the precepts of the law, yet as an innocent creature he was not obliged to the penalties of the law and so suffering was in no wise due upon his own account. And he was without blemish. Had he been a criminal, he could not have been a remedy [i.e. a Saviour]. He had also an alliance with both parties: he could treat with God as partaking of his glory, and be a sacrifice for man as partaking of the infirmities of his [man's] nature. He had a body to bear the stroke due to a victim and a divine nature to sustain him under it. He had a human nature to offer as a sacrifice and a divine nature to render it valuable and infinitely meritorious. Being God and man, he lacked not a fitness to accomplish so great an undertaking. If he had not been man, he could not have been a sacrifice; and if he had not been God, he could not have been a remedy.

It was necessary, in regard of his office of priesthood, that he should be a sacrifice. He was constituted as a priest for ever by an oath (Ps. 110:4). Now he could not be a priest without a sacrifice. A priest and a sacrifice are relatives [related terms]. 'For every high priest taken from among men is ordained for men in things pertaining to God, that he may offer both gifts and sacrifices for sins ... wherefore it is of necessity that this man have somewhat also to offer' (Heb. 5:1; 8:3). As he was a prophet, he was to have a doctrine to teach; as a king, he was to have subjects to govern; as a priest, he was to have a sacrifice to offer. As he was a prophet, he was to deliver something from God to men; as he was a priest, he was to present something for man to

God. As a prophet, he was to teach men obedience to God; as a priest, he was to make God propitious to men. That which he was to offer must be expiatory. That is the proper notion of a sacrifice. The other offerings are termed 'gifts'.

If he had offered the blood of bulls and goats, we had been [would have] in the same case [that] we were in before. The insufficiency of them had not been [would not have been] removed by the dignity of the offerer. They could never in their own nature be proportioned to the dignity of the wronged Sovereign or be adequate to the punishment [which] the criminal had deserved. The impossibility of their taking away sin is positively asserted (Heb. 10:4). The transcendent excellency of the priest could never alter the disproportion between the justice of God provoked by sin and the death of the miserable beast for it. Though the person offering had been greater, the thing offered had been the same. Besides, the offending nature had not [would not have] suffered, but a nature inferior to it. They must have been always offered, the repetition of them must have been continued. And had that been [would that have been] a proper employment for the Son of God, to have been always imbruing his hands in the blood of animals? But a sacrifice must be offered by him (if he did not offer one, he was no priest) and none but [he] himself was a sacrifice worthy to be offered by so great a priest. He offered but once, and it was himself he offered (Heb. 7:27). And this was so spotless (Heb. 9:14) and of such a 'sweet smelling savour' (Eph. 5:2) that it need not again be repeated (Heb. 9:28). His unblemished soul was made an 'offering for sin' (Isa. 53:10). For, being a priest of another kind than the legal [i.e. Levitical] priests, he must have a sacrifice of another kind.

Jesus Christ was then a sacrifice in his human nature.
To this end a body was prepared for him, to be substituted in the place of those sacrifices wherein God had no pleasure: 'Sacrifice and offering thou wouldst not, but a body hast thou prepared me' (Heb. 10:5). [This is] cited out of Psalm 40:6: '[M]ine ears hast thou opened'. Some think that the expression is figurative, the ear being taken for the whole body, because obedience is learned by the ear, [which is] the instrument of hearing the will of another. The will of God was that he should be an offering in this body: 'By the which will we are sanctified through the offering of the body of Jesus Christ once for all' (Heb. 10:10). And his soul was an 'offering for sin' (Isa. 53:10).

The first promise evidenced that though the seed of the woman should tear up the empire of the devil, which by the law he had over sinners, yet it should be by the suffering something from him, by having his heel bruised. There was an obedience to the law to be performed, without which he had not been [would not have been] capable of being a sacrifice. [For] the penalty of the law [had] to be endured, without which he could not be an actual sacrifice. Neither of those could be but [except] in the human nature. Obedience to the law is not consistent with the sovereignty of God [because] according to his divine nature he was under no law. Suffering was impossible to the Deity. It is the property of God to be immutable and impassible. His human nature therefore was the sacrifice; for as he was made of a woman, whereby he took our nature; he was made under the law, whereby he subjected himself to our obedience. He 'redeem[ed] them that were under the law', from our condemnation (Gal. 4:5). He that was to break the serpent's head, that is, to dissolve the power which as

97

an executioner he had from an offended God, was to be the seed of the woman. And this he effected by his death and bloody sacrifice, appeasing the wrath of God, and thereby destroying the power of the jailor which he obtained by the entrance of sin and the curse of the law: '[T]hrough death he might destroy him that had the power of death, that is, the devil' (Heb. 2:14).

This sacrifice was both of soul and body, as the threatening was, 'In the day thou eatest, thou shalt die the death'; that is, be subject to the death and condemnation both of soul and body. As the reward of goodness respects the entire man composed of soul and body, so doth the punishment of sin, which hath corrupted one as well as the other. The sacrifice, therefore, to be offered for the appeasing [of] that wrath and removing [of] the curse was to consist both of soul and body.

That whereby this sacrifice was sanctified, was the divine nature. Every sacrifice was sanctified by the altar (Matt. 23:19). There must be something to add an infinite value to the sufferings of his [Christ's] humanity. This could be nothing but the divine nature, and union with it. Nothing but that which is infinite can confer an infinite value on that which is finite. The infiniteness of dignity resides in the divine nature and essence, and the infiniteness of dignity is as incommunicable as the infiniteness of essence. For it hath its root and foundation in the infiniteness of being, and the one is but the reflection of the other. It is impossible to add a dignity without limits, but one must attribute an essence without bounds. [For example] it is impossible that any thing can possess the lustre and enlivening virtue of the sun, but the sun itself.

The human nature suffered and the divine nature sanctified the humanity, and by reason of this admirable union and the reflection of the divinity upon the humanity, what was done to the human nature upon the cross is ascribed to the whole person. They 'crucified the Lord of glory' (1 Cor. 2:8). And God purchased the church 'with his own blood' (Acts 20:28). It was this [which] made his sufferings acceptable to God, whose justice was to be satisfied, and efficacious for man, whose happiness and commerce [fellowship] with God were to be restored and his needs to be supplied. Thus some interpret Hebrews 9:14: '[T]hrough the eternal Spirit [he] offered himself ... to God', understanding his divine nature, but by virtue of that presented himself to his Father a most acceptable sacrifice. So that he had a human nature to serve for a sacrifice, and an eternal spirit or divine nature wherein he subsisted, from whence that sacrifice derived an infinite dignity, [just] as gold, which hath a lustre of itself, hath a greater when the sun shines full [fully] upon it.

We may see here how Christ was a priest, sacrifice and altar in several respects: a priest in his person, a sacrifice in his humanity, the altar in his divinity. He was the offerer and the sacrifice. Both are expressed, '[He] hath given himself for us an offering' (Eph. 5:2). Active as a priest, passive as a victim: as one, offering; as the other, offered. Upon this account of his blood being offered by his person, he is called God in the act of oblation of his blood for the redemption of the church, 'which he', referring to God, 'hath purchased with his own blood' (Acts 20:28). The Jews and soldiers were not the priests, as some affirm. They were the instruments of slaying him, but not with the intention of a sacrifice. They were instruments in it, but could not force him to it. His death was intended by them; his death was a sacrifice intended by himself. His laying down his life was of himself (John 10:18), which is not meant barely of his death, but of his death as respecting his sheep (v. 15). And indeed, unless it had been voluntary, it had not been [would not have been] savoury [i.e. acceptable].

Upon the sacrifice of Christ, all his other priestly acts depend, and from thence they receive their validity for us.
It is fit therefore we should well understand and often consider this sacrifice, which is the foundation of all our peace and comfort in reference to God. This was the chief thing God eyed in the first declaration of him (Gen. 3:15) in the serpent's bruising his heel. Nothing but this [is here] spoken of. His resurrection was first represented in the safety of Isaac after he was designed to death, and other things not till after that successively. God made the light to dawn upon them by degrees.

(1) *This was the ground of his ascension and entrance into heaven as a priest.* The high priest was not to enter within the veil without blood; what was in the type was to be answered in the antitype. An expiatory sacrifice was necessary to precede his ascension to heaven; the sacrifice must be offered upon the earth, as the legal sacrifices were without. Heaven was no place for slaughter, and with this blood he was to enter. Heaven's gates would have been shut against him without it. Death was the penalty threatened if the legal high priest ventured to step into the holy of holies without blood. The apostle argues from this, 'into the second went the high priest alone once every year, not without blood, which he offered for himself, and for the errors of the people' (Heb. 9:7, 25). According to this type, Christ

by his own blood entered once into the holy place. How and in what order? After he had obtained redemption for us (Heb. 9:12) which is ascribed to his death (v. 15). His entrance into heaven and what he doth for us there, is laid upon the account of [depends on] his death as a sacrifice upon the earth. By virtue of this he went to heaven to present it to God, and apply it to us. And besides, all his royalty and power, whereby we have security and protection from him, depends upon this; for it is because of that obedience to blood and death which he rendered to God, that God has given to him a name above every name and advanced him to a sovereign power: 'Wherefore God also hath highly exalted him' (Phil. 2:8, 9). 'Wherefore' refers to his death (v. 8).

(2) *This is the foundation of his intercession.* There are two functions of Christ's priesthood: oblation and intercession. They are both joined together, but one as precedent to [precedes] the other. The legal high priest, when he had first cut the throat of the sacrifice without upon the day of the anniversary sacrifice, was not esteemed by that act to have completed his propitiation till he had entered into the sanctuary and sprinkled the blood of the sacrifice with his finger. So the propitiation made by our Redeemer was not fully complete till he entered into heaven to exercise his intercession. Yet the oblation precedes the intercession, and the intercession could not be without the oblation. It was with the blood of the victim, and no other blood, he was to enter. Without the oblation, he would have had nothing to present in his intercession. They are placed in this order by the apostle (1 John 2:1, 2). He is first a sacrifice for propitiation, then an advocate for intercession. What he doth as an advocate is grounded upon what he did as

a sacrifice. Were it not so, the apostle's arguing would not be valid, who places our salvation by the life of Christ upon our reconciliation by the death of Christ (Rom. 5:10). Indeed, he could not have been admitted according to the type as an advocate, but as being the high priest, and a high priest he could not have been without a sacrifice.

(3) *This is the foundation of all the grace any have.* The conveyance of all the gracious love of God is through this channel. In redemption by his blood, the riches of the grace of God abounded, and that with the marks of the highest wisdom (Eph. 1:7, 8). All had lain buried from the view of man, and the fruition of men, without this sacrifice. This did commend his love as well as satisfy his justice. His wrath had not been [would not have been] appeased, nor his grace drawn out to us, without it. Nor could the Redeemer lay any claim to any grace and mercy for those for whom he came, unless he had suffered for them as well as taken flesh for them. His 'offering himself' (Isa. 53:10-12) precedes his having a seed. The being [existence] and beauty of his seed depend upon the efficacy of his meritorious sacrifice. The offering [of] his soul goes before the pardon of our sin; the payment of the ransom before the sprinkling [of] it on us; the sealing [of] the covenant before the making good the covenant; his sufferings before his triumph; and the streams of his blood before the treasures of his grace. Upon the account of this sacrifice we enjoy the presence of God, protection against the enemies of our salvation, and receive the blessings necessary for our souls.

By all this it appears [plainly] that Christ is a sacrifice. This was his intent in coming. His death as a sacrifice was his intention in the assumption of our flesh; the prophecies predicted it, the types represented it; this he pursued, for this he thirsted. The accomplishment of this fiery baptism was the matter of his longing, his thoughts were never [far] off from it, his will shrunk not from it. When his human will showed some reluctance, he quickly returned to its fixedness. Nothing could deter him, nothing could divert him. When he undertook to be mediator, he undertook to be a sacrifice, as a thing necessarily annexed to that office for the honour of God's justice and the preservation of the rights of his sacred law. Upon which account, when the apostle speaks of this Mediator, he adds with the same breath, 'Who gave himself a ransom for all' (1 Tim. 2:5, 6). After the title of Mediator follows the 'blood of sprinkling' (Heb. 12:24). A Mediator he was by means of his 'death' (Heb. 9:15). It is with good reason, therefore, that in our creed there is so quick a passage from the nativity of Christ to his passion, without any mention of the acts of his life, because he was incarnate that he might be crucified.

The essence of a sacrifice consisted, firstly in the slaying or destroying it, and secondly, in the offering it to God. Both were done in Christ.

In the slaying or destroying it. The shedding of the blood, the seat of the spirits [i.e. the life], which are the instruments of action,[7] was necessary to an expiatory sacrifice. The scape-goat indeed is called a sacrifice (Lev. 16:5) which was not slain in the temple, nor burnt, but sent into the wilderness; and, as the Jews tell us, destroyed by being thrown down a rock, to which purpose men were appointed: who were to give notice of it by some signals from hill to hill, at

---

7   By this phrase Charnock evidently means that the activity of animals depends on the supply of strength which is through its blood. Ed.

a convenient distance. Before this notice [intimation], the congregation at Jerusalem did not dissolve [disperse]. But the other expiatory sacrifices were devoured by fire, since fire is the highest representation in the world of the justice of God. The sufferings of Christ extended to soul and body. He was scorched by the wrath of God (Ps. 22:14-19). His soul was poured out to death (Isa. 53:12), alluding to the blood of the sacrifices poured out. And his human nature [was] dissolved by the separation of the soul and body.

In the offering [of] it to God. Oblation to God was a main part of a sacrifice, so 'Christ ... hath given himself ... to God' (Eph. 5:2). To God as essentially considered, whereby the whole right of government and dominion was acknowledged [as] belonging to God. Had the death of Christ been only for [an] example, it had not been [would not have been] offered to God, who did not need any example to be set for him. The fact therefore that it was offered to God proves that it was a sacrifice.

Part 3: Christ was sacrificed for us

The original word, when joined with suffering for another, always signifies in another's stead and place. It is so used, 'For a good man some would even dare to die' (Rom. 5:7), that is, instead of a good man, to free him from the death he was designed to, not only for his sake. So 'being made a curse for us' (Gal. 3:13) that is, in our stead, suffering the curse due to us for our sins. He is called the Lamb of God in regard of God's designation of him: our lamb, our passover, in regard of his substitution in our place. As he died to appease the wrath of God, his death referred to the justice of God; as that justice flamed out against us, his death referred to us. He was a screen between the heat of wrath and the sufferings of the creature; a Mediator respecting God, for his satisfaction and glory; respecting us, for our reparation [recovery] and grace.

Christ could not be a sacrifice for himself.
The Messiah was to be cut off, but 'not for himself' (Dan. 9:26): he needed no sacrifice for himself as the other high priests did; they were sinners, he was harmless. They being encompassed with infirmities needed or ought to offer sacrifices for themselves (Heb. 5:2, 3). He was 'a lamb without blemish ... Who did no sin, neither was guile found in his mouth' (1 Pet. 1:19; 2:22) nor did he ever do any thing displeasing to his Father (John 8:29). He needed no glory to be purchased for him, for he was from eternity happy in the same essence with the Father, being 'God blessed for ever' (Rom. 9:5), having the command over all, and lacking nothing to a perfect blessedness. The sacrifices which were types of him could not be for themselves; they were not capable of sinning since they lacked a rational nature, and therefore a sinful nature. A beast was not capable of sin because not capable of a law, and therefore its blood was not due for any sin of its own. Christ had no sin, none actual, 'no guile [was] found in his mouth' (1 Pet. 2:22), nor original, that was stopped [prevented] by his extraordinary conception by the Holy Ghost, which rendered him immaculate [sinless].

Sacrifices implied this.
They had a relation to the offerer, and were substituted in his place. The substitution of the sacrifice in the place of the offenders was always supposed by the heathen; hence did the offering of human victims arise, their opinion being that they could not present to God a nobler creature in their stead than one of their own nature. The notion of

all sacrifices was that they were in the place of a sinner, to appease the offending Deity, and exempt the guilty person from punishment. And the actions about the Jewish sacrifices manifested this. The offerer laid his hand upon the head of the beast, signifying by that ceremony its consecration to God, and [thus] owning [confessing] the translation [transfer] of his guilt upon that creature and putting it 'in the place where they kill the burnt offering before the Lord: it is a sin offering' (Lev. 4:24, 29). And in this action of laying on hands, both hands and with all their strength, as the Jews tell us, confession of sin was made by the presenter of the sacrifice, which signified also the disburdening of his guilt upon the head of the victim. By those actions was manifested a transferring of sin from the offender to the sacrifice, and of the death due to the criminal in like manner.

Besides, the pouring out of the blood, wherein the soul [i.e. life – not, of course an immortal soul, as in the case of humans] of the beast was supposed to be, was destined for the expiation of the sin of the soul of the offerer (Lev. 17:11, 14); not that the blood is properly the soul, but because the vital spirits, which are the instrument of action and conveying the virtue of the soul to particular members [of the body], are seated in the blood.

The whole economy of Christ is expressed in the whole scripture to have a relation to us.

All things preparatory to his sufferings were for us. Some were first given to him, before he was given for them (John 17:9); he took flesh for us, 'unto us a child is born' (Isa. 9:6); for he has a fullness of grace in his human nature (John 1:16); for our sakes he dedicated himself, that we might be sanctified (John 17:19); for us he gave himself (Gal. 2:20); in the very moment of his sufferings our iniquities were laid upon him, that health by his stripes might be derived [conveyed] to us.

Christ was a common person[8] for us, as the scape-goat was common to the whole congregation (Lev. 16:21), representing all of them. Christ was a common person for us, as Adam was, to whom in this respect he is compared: '[W]ho is', that is, Adam, 'the figure of him that was to come' (Rom. 5:14). The apostle compares one Adam and one Christ. He illustrates the condition and the actions of the one by the condition and actions of the other. What happened to us by Adam is compared to what happened to us by Christ.

This typicalness of Adam cannot be in any other regard than as he was a common person, representing all that were in his loins by natural generation. In this regard, Christ is called the second man: 'The first man is of the earth, earthy; the second man is the Lord from heaven' (1 Cor. 15:47). Not that he was the second man born in the world, for many ages were run before his incarnation: but the second common root in the world. As when Adam, being the first root of mankind in a natural way, fell, the curse came upon him and all his posterity, and the standing punishments pronounced against him did reach and were meant of [for] all his posterity (Gen. 3:19). This was so not only of Adam as a person but of Adam as a representative, and so of all those who were not yet born into the world. As we sinned in Adam as a common root of natural generation, so we

---

8   Charnock means that Christ was a public person whose office involved
     him in acting on behalf of others. Ed.

were all sacrificed in Christ as a common head of all that are in him by a spiritual union. The one merited death and damnation for all that descend from him, the other life and salvation for all that believe in him.

Our sins were imputed to him as to a sacrifice.
Christ the just is put in the place of the unjust, to suffer for them (1 Pet. 3:18). Christ is said to bear sin, as a sacrifice bears sin (Isa. 53:10, 12). His soul was made an offering for it. But sin was so laid upon the victims, as that it was imputed to them in a judicial account [manner] according to the ceremonial law, and typically expiated by them. Christ had not [would not have] taken away our sins as Mediator, had he not borne the punishment of them. As a surety, 'he hath made him to be sin for us' (2 Cor. 5:21), and he bare our sins, which is evident by the kind of death he suffered, not only sharp and shameful but accursed, having a sense of God's wrath linked to it.

(1) Imputation cannot be understood of the *infection of sin*. The filth of our nature was not transmitted to him. Though he was made sin, yet he was not made a sinner by any infusion or transplantation of sin into his nature. It was impossible his holiness could be defiled with our filth.

(2) But our sin was the *meritorious cause of his punishment*. All those phrases, that 'Christ died for our sins' (1 Cor. 15:3) and was 'delivered [to death] for our offences' (Rom. 4:25) clearly import [mean] sin to be the meritorious cause of the punishment [which] Christ endured. Sin cannot be said to be the cause of punishment, but [except] by way of merit. If Christ had not been just, he had not been [would not have been] capable of suffering for us; had we not been unjust, we had not [would not have] merited any suffering

for ourselves, much less for another. Our unrighteousness put us under a necessity of a sacrifice, and his righteousness made him fit to be one. What was the cause of the desert of suffering for ourselves was the meritorious cause of the sufferings of the Redeemer after he put himself in our place. The sin of the offerer merited the death of the sacrifice presented in his stead.

(3) Our sins were charged upon him *in regard of their guilt*. Our sins are so imputed to him as that they are not imputed to us (2 Cor. 5:19), and not imputed to us because he was 'made a curse for us' (Gal. 3:13). He bore our sins, as to the punishment, is granted. If he were an offering for them, they must in a judicial way be charged upon him. If by being made sin, be understood a sacrifice for sin (which indeed is the true intent of the word sometimes in scripture), sin was then legally transferred on the antitype, as it was on the types in the Jewish service by the ceremony of laying on of hands and confessing of sin, after which the thing so dedicated became accursed and, though it was in itself innocent, yet was guilty in [the] sight of [the] law and as a substitute. In the same manner was Christ accounted. So on the contrary, believers are personally guilty, but by virtue of the satisfaction of this sacrifice imputed to them, they are judically counted innocent. Christ, who never sinned, is put in such a state as if he had; and we, who have always sinned, are put into such a state by him as if we never had. As we are made righteous in him, so he was made sin for us.

Now, as justifying righteousness is not inherent in us, but imputed to us, so our condemning sin was not inherent in Christ, but imputed to him. There would else [otherwise] be no consistency in the antithesis: 'he hath made him to be sin for us, who knew no sin' (2 Cor. 5:21). He knew no sin, yet he became sin. It seems to carry it [the idea] further than only the bearing [of] the punishment of sin. He was by law charged in our stead with the guilt of sin. Our iniquities were laid upon him (Isa. 53:6). The prophet had spoken (v. 5) of Christ bearing the chastisement of our peace, the punishment of our sin, and then seems to declare the ground of that, which consisted in God's imputation of sin to him in laying upon him the iniquities of us all. What iniquities? Our goings astray, our turnings every one to his own way. He made him to be that sin which he knew not, but he knew the punishment of sin. The knowledge of that was the end of his coming. He came to lay down his life a ransom for many. He knew not sin by an experimental inherency [something in his own nature], but he knew it by judicial imputation. He knew it not in regard of the spots, but he knew it in regard of the guilt following upon the judgment of God. He was righteous in his person, but not in the sight of the law pronounced righteous as our Surety till after his sacrifice, when he was 'taken from prison and from judgment' (Isa. 53:8). Till he had paid the debt, he was accounted as a debtor to God.

The apostle distinguishes his second coming from his first by this, 'he [shall] appear the second time without sin unto salvation' (Heb. 9:28). It is not meant of the filth of sin, for so he appeared at first without sin. But [he will appear] without the guilt of sin which he had at his first coming derived or taken upon himself to satisfy for and remove from the sinner. He shall appear without sin to be imputed, without punishment to be inflicted. At the time of his first coming he appeared with sin, with sin charged upon him, as our Surety arrested for our criminal debts. He pawned his life for the lives which we had forfeited. He suffered the penalty due by law that we might have a deliverance free by grace. In his first coming he represented our persons as an undertaker [proxy] for us. Our sins were therefore laid upon him. In his second coming he represents God as a deputy, and so no sin can be charged upon him.

He cannot well be supposed to suffer for our sins, if our sins in regard of their guilt be not supposed to be charged upon him. How could he die, if he were not reputed a sinner? Had he not first had a relation to our sin, he could not in justice have undergone our punishment. He must in the order of justice be [either] supposed a sinner really, or [else] by imputation. Since he was not a sinner really, he was so by imputation. How can we conceive [that] he should be made a curse for us, if that which made us accursed had not been first charged upon him? It is as much against divine justice to inflict punishment where there is no sin, as it is to spare an offender who has committed a crime or to 'clear the guilty'. This God will by no means do (Exod. 34:7). The consideration of a crime precedes the sentence, either upon an offender or his surety. We cannot conceive how divine justice should inflict the punishment, had it not first considered him under guilt.

Though the first designation of the Redeemer to a suretyship or sacrifice for us was an act of God's sovereignty, yet the inflicting punishment after that designation and our Saviour's acceptation of it was an act of God's justice, and so declared to be, 'To declare ... his righteousness: that he might be just' (Rom. 3:26), that he might declare his justice in justification, his justice to his law. Can this highest declaration of justice be founded upon an unjust act? Would that have been justice or injustice to Christ, for God to lay his wrath upon the Son of his love, one whose person was always dear to him, always pleased him, had he not stood as a sinner regarded so by law in our stead, and suffered that sin, which was the ruin of mankind, to be cast with all the weight of it upon his innocent shoulders? After, by his own act, he had engaged for [made himself responsible for] our debt, God in justice might demand of him every farthing, which without that undertaking and putting himself in our stead could not be done. This submission of his and compliance with it [readiness to suffer for it] is expressed twice, by his not opening his mouth (Isa. 53:7); and no wrong is done to a voluntary undertaker [i.e. sufferer].

Add this too. It is from his standing in our stead as guilty that the benefit of his death redounds to us. His death had had [would have had] no relation to us had not our sin been lawfully adjudged to be his; nor can we challenge an acquittance [plead for pardon] at the hands of God for our debts if they were not *our* debts that he paid on the cross. '[H]e was wounded for our transgressions, he was bruised for our iniquities' (Isa. 53:5). The laying hands on the head of the sin-offering was necessary to make it a sacrifice for the offender, without which ceremony it might have been a slain but not a sacrificed beast. The transferring our iniquities upon him must in some way precede his being bruised for them, which could not be any other way than by imputation whereby he was constituted by God a debtor in our stead to bear the punishment of our sin. Since he was made sin for us, our sin was in a sort [manner] made his; he was made sin without sin; he knew the guilt without knowing the filth; he felt the punishment without being touched with the pollution. Since death was the wages of sin and passed as a penalty for a violated law (Rom. 6:23) it could not righteously be inflicted on him, if sin had not first been imputed to him. In his own person he was in the arms of his Father's love; as he represented our sinful persons, he felt the strokes of his Father's wrath.

The sufferings of this sacrifice are imputed unto us.
He took our sins upon himself as if he had sinned and gave us the benefit of his sufferings as if we had actually suffered and satisfied; he 'offered one sacrifice for sins for ever' (Heb. 10:12), that is to take away sin; if you compare it with verse 11, to remove the wrath due to us by reason of iniquity was the end he aimed at. As our sins were imputed to him for punishment, so his sufferings are imputed to us for acceptation [acceptance]: 'he hath made us accepted in the beloved. In whom we have redemption through his blood' (Eph. 1:6, 7). Christ had the relation of an undertaker [Surety] for us and we the relation of debtors to God. Our debts then being charged upon him, his payment must be imputed to us. The Surety and the principal are legally regarded as one person; so are the representative and the persons represented by him. As Adam and all mankind were as one person, and as all Israel were called Jacob from the common root of them, so Christ and believers are as one person. And what he did is as if a believer himself did it, [just] as the suffering of the sacrifice was accepted in lieu of the life of the sinner.

By the stripes of our sacrifice, 'we are healed' (Isa. 53:5). An exchange is made, stripes to him, health to us. He was made a curse, that we might be freed 'from the curse' (Gal. 3:13). The first thing rising upon faith from the sufferings of Christ is a non-imputation of sin, 'not imputing their trespasses unto them' (2 Cor. 5:19). They are not imputed to a believer, because borne by the undertaker [substitute] for him. The main end [aim] of his death as a sacrifice was to communicate a righteousness to us: 'if righteousness come by the law, then Christ is dead in vain' (Gal. 2:21). If this were the main or only thing that would make the death of Christ a mere vanity, then the great and main end of his death was to procure a complete righteousness for us: a righteousness whereby he was to be glorified, a righteousness whereby we might be justified. His sufferings procured it, his resurrection ensured it.

All the world stands guilty before God; they cannot present God with a righteousness of their own, commensurate to the law. Not one act any man can do can bear proportion to it. All strength to do any thing suitable to it was lost in Adam. Since no righteousness of our own can justify, it must be the righteousness of the Son of God which must be imputed to him. It is accepted by God for us, and it is accounted by God to us: 'he hath made him to be sin for us, who knew no sin; that we might be made the righteousness of God in him' (2 Cor. 5:21). Sin was in us, but charged upon [reckoned to] Christ; righteousness is in Christ, and imputed to us. Therefore the apostle adds him to signify, that it is not our own righteousness, but another's, not [a thing] inherent in us, but imputed to us.

The crediting of these sufferings to us, arises:

(1) *From the dignity of the person undertaking to be a sacrifice for us and the union of our nature with his.* He assumed our nature that he might be a common [i.e. representative] person and stand in our stead. He had not been [would not have been] a fit representative of us without it. But the main consideration is 'the fullness of the Godhead

bodily' (Col. 2:9) and his being the man, God's fellow (Zech. 13:7). For this reason what he did and suffered in our stead became, according to the value of the person performing it, infinitely meritorious for those for whom he suffered, being infinitely more than all the obedience of men and angels, and more meritorious of happiness than sin could be of misery. As infinite sin deserves an infinite punishment because it receives its aggravation from the dignity of the person against whom it is committed, so the sufferings of Christ, though finite in regard of his human nature, received an infinite value from the infiniteness of his person, equivalent to the debts of all that come to him. Sin is finite in regard to the subject, infinite in regard to the great God against whom it is; the sufferings of Christ are infinite in regard of the subject and infinitely please the Governor of the world unto whom the offering is made. And therefore are of more force to convey a righteousness and beauty to the creature than sin is to convey guilt and filth; though 'sin abounded, grace did much more abound' (Rom. 5:20).

(2) *From union with this infinite person by faith.* All believers have a communion with him in his death: 'if one died for all, then were all dead' (2 Cor. 5:14). All were accounted as dying and bearing the wrath of God by God's reckoning that death to them. As the sin of Adam is imputed to all his natural posterity as being one with him in his loins, so are the sufferings of Christ imputed to all his spiritual seed (Rom. 5:18) as being one with him in a real union. Hence we are said to be 'crucified with him' (Rom. 6:6) and risen with him (Eph. 2:6) as in the person representing us; as if the same wrath endured by Christ had been endured by us

and the same acquittance given to Christ had been given to us by God together with him. For all his meritorious passions were endured by him in the name of his elect and for their use, and are fully belonging, in the fruit and benefit of them, to every believer. What Christ as a Mediator did personally do is credited in the benefit of it to the Church and is reckoned to every member of his body. We are made, every one of us that believe, the righteousness of God in him. Well, then, Christ bearing our iniquities is the cause of our justification: '[B]y his knowledge shall my righteous servant justify many; for he shall bear their iniquities' (Isa. 53:11). If our sin had not been imputed to him, his righteousness could not be accounted to us. The commutation [exchange] is clear. He first bears our iniquities that we might partake of his righteousness.

Application: If Christ be a sacrifice:

1. *We may see the miserable blindness of the Jews in expecting the Messiah as a temporal conqueror.*

The Jews wait for such a one to this day. The promises represent spiritual deliverances under temporal grandeurs, not to raise carnal hopes, but spiritual apprehensions. Yet are there not multitudes of places [i.e. Old Testament texts] which speak of sufferings, misery, death? Is not his heel to be bruised, are not his garments to be parted and a restoration to be made by him of what he took not away? Are not the sacrifices of the law to be perfected, his soul to be made an offering for sin, wounds made for transgression, his hands and his feet to be pierced? It was not by slaying the bodies of men that he was to make reconciliation for the iniquities of men (Dan. 9:24). How can he be a conqueror of kingdoms, who is to be cut off, and the city where he was to be destroyed as with a flood, and the desolations of it to be determined [to quote the language of Daniel]? Verse 26: penally 'cut off', as the word signifies (Lev. 17:4), as one was cut off that had no sacrifice allowed for him. The right apprehensions of the promises concerning the Messiah in the Old Testament, what he was to be, what he was to do, cannot let you be ignorant of him in the New. How do those poor people [i.e. unbelieving Jews] overturn at once the whole design of that divine law [which] they seem to reverence in the highest degree! What blindness will seize upon the hearts of men, even under the oracles of God, if the Spirit of God does not vouchsafe to [undertake to] enlighten them?

2. If Christ is a sacrifice it shows the necessity of a satisfaction to the justice of God and a higher satisfaction than men could perform.
Blood must satisfy justice, and no blood but that of the Son of God could be a sufficient and valuable propitiation. If mere mercy could or would have pardoned, it might have done it with or without the blood of the poor creatures mangled under the law. But, alas! neither the blood of those nor the blood of a rational creature could take away sin. Less than death, justice could not demand; death was settled by the immediate order of God as the penalty of the law. The law then after transgression could not be vindicated in its honour without death. A God of infinite goodness delights not in shedding the blood of his creatures, nor can we suppose him to be pleased with the effusion [outpouring] of the blood of animals. The institution of the legal sacrifices could not be exemplary to man. What virtue could the pangs of a dying beast represent to him? No other ends

[objectives] can be imagined but an acknowledgment of guilt, the desert of sin, the debt of death, the necessity of a higher satisfaction, and the raising [of] them up to a faith in the promise of God. [It indicated] that another, [more valuable] valuable, sacrifice should be put in the room of the sinner to take away that sin which the blood of beasts and the eternal groans of men were not able to remove.

3. *Christ, as sacrificed, is the true and immediate object of faith.* We are [have] revolted from God and are made incapable of performing the terms of the first covenant. The precepts of the law are too holy for our corrupt nature, the penalties of the law too grievous to be borne by our feeble nature. A remedy must be looked for. When the venom of sin begins to work in the conscience, and the thunder of the law alarms it to judgment, and the punishment due to sin is presented in the horrors of it, the question immediately is: Is there any remedy? If so, where? How can forgiveness of sin be attained. The only remedy is proposed in Christ, and Christ as a sacrifice. It is not Christ risen or ascended or exalted; not Christ only as the Son of God or the head of angels; not Christ as the Creator of the world or by whom all things consist. But Christ as answering the terms of the first covenant, as disarming justice. And this he did as a sacrifice. By this he bore the curse, by this he broke down the partition-wall, by this he joined apostate man and an offended God. This is what true faith pitches on [rests on], daily revolves [thinks about] and daily applies to.

This is the first object of the soul: Christ made sin, Christ bearing the punishment, Christ substituted in the room of the offender. His resurrection and ascension come in afterwards to ascertain the comfort. His being a sacrifice is the foundation of his being an Advocate, a Prince, a Saviour to give repentance and remission of sins. Hence it is the foundation of peace in ourselves. This is that which pacifies God, and only what pacifies God can pacify conscience. This death as a sacrifice purchased our comfort because it purchased the Comforter. Christ begged not [prayed not for] the Spirit before he died (John 16:7). He assures them the Spirit could not come unless he himself went. And he could not have gone with any success to heaven if he had not shed his blood. Justice would have stopped his entrance: 'Ought not Christ to have suffered these things, and to enter into his glory?' (Luke 24:26). Suffering was to precede his glory.

Besides, our comfort lies in his being an Advocate. But how is he an Advocate? With his blood in his hands. It is by his blood he speaks in heaven, and by his blood faith speaks to God. He paid the debt in his suffering and pleads the payment in his glory. The payment went before the plea in order of nature, and our eyeing the payment precedes our eyeing the plea in order of faith. Both respect God as the Ruler. Christ without his garments rolled in blood could not be answerable to God nor acceptable to a sinner. Faith is therefore called 'faith in his blood' (Rom. 3:25). As faith is the instrument of justification, so it must eye the cause of our justification, and under that notion wherein it is the cause. This is no other than Christ as groaning and offering up himself to God a ransom, a righteousness for many.

The curse upon Adam is the lash wherewith an angry conscience scourges a sinner. The freedom from this curse is only found in the vengeance [which] God exacted of the Redeemer for the sins of all that return to him by repentance. Both the death and resurrection of Christ concur [work together] to the same end, namely, our justification (Rom. 14:9). But [they do so] in different manners: his death as the meritorious cause, his resurrection as declarative of the sufficiency of his death to that end, that as the Son of God and Surety of men, he had performed whatsoever he undertook in his being a sacrifice. But the first act of relying faith is about him as a bloody victim. As often as the Israelites were stung by the fiery serpents, they were to look up for health to the serpent lifted up, a type and emblem of the death of Christ. Upon every sin of a believer, the sacrifice is pleaded in heaven by the Priest and ought in the remembrance of it to be renewed in the repeated acts of our faith.

4. *It is no true opinion [i.e. it is a false idea] that Christ died only for an example.*
Wounded he was for the transgressions of Isaiah's time, when his example could reach only those that came after him. But the credit of his sufferings upon his promise to undergo them might and did reach the first ages of the world. The expressions in Isaiah 53 found his death higher than a bare pattern or a testimony to the truth. The notion of expiation of sin was always implied in the notion of a sacrifice, even among the heathens. When they parted with the dearest first-born of their bodies to Moloch,[91] it was not for an example, but 'for the sin of my soul' (Micah 6:7). As Christ was the Son of God sent, he was a testimony of the love of God; as he was a sacrifice, he was our ransom from the curse of the law.

---

9   A Pagan God of the Old Testament times whose worship involved the cruel sacrifice of children. Ed.

5. *Comfort to every true believer.*

He was sacrificed for us. God counted him a sinner [i.e. guilty] for our sakes, that he might count us righteous for his sake.

(a) Christ has been sacrificed for them and he has been accepted for them. He is no more to be made sin. Iniquity [is] no more to be charged upon him. His next appearance will be without the imputation of sin for the conferring salvation (Heb. 9:28) with all the bonds of a believer's sins cancelled. He is pronounced God's righteous servant, and from this declaration of his righteousness and the true and believing knowledge of it does our justification arise (Isa. 53:11). Had it not been a perfect sacrifice, it could never have wrought such complete effects or 'hath perfected for ever them that are sanctified' (Heb. 10:14). He has gone with the smoke of his sacrifice to heaven and was well entertained [received], which is a signification [an indication] of the completeness and perfection of his righteousness for man (John 16:10).

The pure and piercing eye of divine Justice could not perceive a spot in him. Had any blemish been, it could not have escaped an infinite knowledge. Nor could the justice of God, in turning over all the registers of the debts owing from the creatures, perceive one that might not be cancelled upon the value of this payment, if the creature did not negligently or wilfully refuse his own delivery [deliverance] and prefer his debts and captivity to it. It was a sacrifice offered according to God's heart, with which his soul was infinitely well pleased. The person of the Son of God made every gaping wound, every panting groan and doleful agony pleasing to God and profitable for us. The Godhead united to the manhood put an inexpressible value upon every pang. Not that every pang or the least drop of blood was sufficient for our redemption. The law required death and death must be suffered. But all those passions preceding his death were meritorious in conjunction with his death.

(b) This sacrifice unites all the attributes of God together for a believer's interest. The floodgates of mercy are opened and the fire of justice confined in its flames. The flames of the one centre in Christ so that the streams of the other might flow down to us. Rivers of mercy do not quench the flames of justice nor the flames of justice suck up the rivers of mercy. As the sacrificing Christ is a vengeance against sin, it is an act of justice; as it is a means of remission of the sins of those for whom he was sacrificed, it is an act of mercy to the creature. Both Justice and Mercy join hands to help the fallen creature up. God is just in being merciful, and merciful in being just. So we well may cry aloud with the psalmist, 'Gracious is the LORD, and righteous' (Ps. 116:5). Justice struck the sacrifice that the streams of mercy might have a fuller scope. Compassion helped justice to a satisfaction more honourable than could have been had from creatures; and justice helped mercy to a fuller and more illustrious exercise of itself than ever it could have had without it. Justice is now a second to mercy; of an [from being an] antagonist it is become an advocate. God must be unjust if he be not merciful to a believer. Since our High Priest has been faithful to God, God will not be unfaithful to him or those for whom he offered up himself. Happy must he be, that has mercy supplicating, and justice itself pleading for him.

(c) This sacrifice is of eternal virtue. The virtue of the sacrifice is parallel to the office of his priesthood. A priest and a sacrifice are relatives [correlatives]. The immutable oath then that constituted him a priest for ever settles for ever the value and virtue of the sacrifice. For without a sacrifice he could not be a priest. His office would expire if the virtue of his sacrifice did. They eternally lived together in conjunction. It is the 'blood of the everlasting covenant' (Heb. 13:20). It is an everlasting covenant because of an everlasting blood whereby it was settled. The ground of its prevalence is, that it was not the sacrifice of a mere man, but of God (Heb. 9:14).

(d) The effects of this sacrifice therefore are perfect, glorious and eternal. It is our deliverance from wrath, the scorchings of hell and terrors of punishment. The purity of this sacrifice expiates the impurities of our services. No sin so great, but the value of this sacrifice, believed in, can answer it [atone for]. The highest sin is the transgression of the law, and this is the satisfaction of the whole penalty of the law. Sin is an offence against God and this sacrifice is the highest pleasure to him. None of our sins can be so great as all those that met upon the back of this innocent Lamb. It is enough to cross every book of accounts [i.e. cancel all debts]: 'Who shall lay any thing to the charge of God's elect? It is God that justifieth. ...[and] Christ that died' (Rom. 8:33, 34); 'There is therefore now no condemnation to them which are in Christ Jesus ... God sending his own Son in the likeness of sinful flesh, and for sin, condemned sin in the flesh' (Rom. 8:1, 3). Paul does not say, 'No desert of condemnation' for that there is. He does not say, 'No condemnation because of something done by themselves'. No, but because of something done by Christ who has obliterated the blood red roll of sin and curses by his own blood. God will not refuse it to any man who believingly pleads it; he will not be unjust to the true value of it, nor to his own ordination [appointment]. If it be unrighteous for

God to 'forget your work and labour of love' (Heb. 6:10), it will be so to forget the obedience of his Son, and the person interested in it. God was not more ready to bruise him for us, than to apply the plaster [remedy] of his blood to us.

How great, then, is the happiness of a believer on the account of this sacrifice! Whatsoever is lost by the sin of the first Adam is gained by the sacrifice of the second. With what boldness may we enter into the holiest with this blood of Jesus in our hands and hearts (Heb. 10:19)!

6. *We must then lay hold on this sacrifice.*

The people were to be sprinkled with the blood of the sacrifice (Exod. 24:8). So must we with the blood of our Lamb. Thus only can it save us (1 Pet. 1:2). Thus is our Saviour described by this part of his office: 'So shall he sprinkle many nations' (Isa. 52:15). Our guilt cannot look upon a consuming fire without a propitiatory sacrifice; our services are blemished, so that they will rather provoke his justice than merit his mercy; we must have something to put a stop to a just fury, expiate an infinite guilt and perfume our unsavoury services. Here it is in Christ, but there must be faith in us. Faith is as necessary by the ordination of God in a way of instrumentality as the grace of God in a way of efficiency and the blood of Christ in a way of meritoriousness of our justification. All must concur: the will of God the offended Governor, the will of the sacrificing Mediator and the will of the offender. This will must be a real will, an active operative will, not a faint will. We must have a faith to justify our persons, and we must have an active sincerity to justify the reality of our faith. Christ was real in his sacrifice; God was real in the acceptation of it; we must be real in believing it.

Rocks and mountains cannot secure them that neglect so great a sacrifice, that regard this atoning blood as an unholy thing. It is as dreadful for men to have this sacrifice smoking against them and this blood calling for vengeance on them, as it is comfortable to have it pleaded for them and sprinkled on them. Why will any then despise and neglect a necessary sovereign remedy ready at hand? Is it excusable, that when we should have brought the sacrifice ourselves or ourselves have been the sacrifice, we should slight him who hath voluntarily been a sacrifice for us, and cherish a hell merited by our sin rather than accept of a righteousness purchased at no less rate than the blood of God? This sacrifice is full of all necessary virtue to save us; but the blood of it must be sprinkled upon our souls by faith. Without this we shall remain in our sins, under the wrath of God, and sword of vengeance.

7. *We must be enemies to sin, since Christ was a sacrifice for it.* Unless sin die in us, we cannot have an evidence that this sacrifice was slain for us. He that hath an interest in Christ's blood must be planted 'in the likeness of his death' (Rom. 6:5). We are highly unjust if we will not sacrifice a beloved sin for him who sacrificed a precious life of more value than heaven and earth for us. We should empty ourselves of our filth since he emptied himself of his glory. The very expression, 'sacrificed for us', carries a force and a spirit in it to animate us to this. We must be friends to the duties God enjoins us. It is ingratitude to put him off with a shred of our souls, or a grain of service, who became a holocaust [a burnt-sacrifice wholly consumed] for us. Scanty services are fit only for a scanty sacrifice. As God shows in this sacrifice his compassions to the sinner, so

he declares the certainty and terror of his penalties upon the obstinate rebel. If the Son of God, undertaking to be a sacrifice, was not preserved from death upon the account of his filiation [his being a Son], men cannot expect but to sink under it upon the account of their rebellion.

Well then, let us not look upon the least sin without horror, since it is a crime not to be expiated by any lower price than an infinite blood. It should cause us to mourn also for sin. It was our unrighteousness that made Christ's back and his soul to suffer; he had never felt the wrath of his Father if we had not broken the law of his Father. When the death of Christ our sacrifice comes into our thoughts, the remembrance of our sins should bear it company. We should never consider that Christ died, but we should join also with sorrow at the consideration of that for which he died.

3

The Voluntariness of Christ's Death

And walk in love, as Christ also hath loved us, and hath
given himself for us an offering and a sacrifice to God for
a sweetsmelling savour.
Ephesians 5:2

The exhortation in this verse to a mutual love depends upon what the apostle had urged in the end of the former chapter, where he had endeavoured to persuade them to [show] a kindness and tender-heartedness to one another, and backed it [i.e. supported his argument] by the pattern [which] God had set them in his pardoning grace. And in verse 1 of this chapter, he extends that motive to all other duties and draws a general maxim for their observance. He says that they ought to imitate God in all things imitable by a creature: 'Be ye therefore followers of God, as dear children' (v. 1). Consider the great example which God hath set you, and that you have obligations to him, not only as your God but as your Father. So imitate him, not only as creatures but as children. Express in your lives those admirable perfections which he has engraven on you by regeneration, and especially his patience and meekness in bearing, and his love and kindness in pardoning those who injure you.

Those who lay claim to a relation to God without imitation of him are not children but bastards. They may be of his family by instruction but not by descent. There is no implantation in Christ without an imitation both of the Creator and Redeemer.

Paul states the exhortation in this verse: 'walk in love'. Let the perpetual tenor of your lives be in love. Paul here argues from the example of Christ, as earlier he had done from the example of God the Father. Christ, when on earth, had urged the same example on his disciples before his departure from them: 'I have given you an example, that ye should do as I have done to you' (John 13:15). He amplifies this example of the love of Christ: 1. From the effect of it: His passion; 2. The manner of it as voluntary: 'hath given'; 3. The subject of it: 'himself'; 4. The end of it: 'a sacrifice'; 5. The event and fruit of it.

'[A] sweetsmelling savour'. A fragrant odour, which by a metalepsis [figure of speech] is put for the appeasing of God, since it has a wonderful force to appease the wrath of God which was inflamed against us. The most generous example to imitate is the person of our Saviour; the most efficacious motive to persuade to that imitation is the sacrifice of our Saviour. The course of our lives ought to be in love, not only an act, a spurt, but a walk. '[A]s Christ also hath loved us'. We are to do it similarly though we cannot do it equally. We cannot equal the stature of Christ's affection, but we may draw in our life features like to his [i.e. copy Christ].

The latter words [of Eph. 5:2] are the subject of this discourse: 'loved us'. This is the first spring of all the actions of Christ towards us, and the passion of Christ for us. There could be no other motive as it respected [with regard to] us. Our misery might excite his pity, but his affection produced his passion. He loved us, as God, in common with his Father; he loved us, as man, by a participation of our nature. In this love, there is his divine will as a priest and his human will as a sacrifice. He pitied us while we were insensibly hurried down by the devil to a gulf of perdition. Love was the only impulse. Love excited him, love prepared him, love sent him, love offered him. The highest assurance of his love was the loss of his life. The excellency of the fruit shows the goodness of the tree.

'[H]ath given himself'. He was given by God, yet he offered himself. There was a joint consent: 'The Son can do nothing of himself, but what he seeth the Father do' (John 5:19). It is spoken after the manner of men, as sons learn of their fathers, and imitate them in their actions. Christ's giving himself implies the Father's giving him.

'[H]imself'. He was both the priest and the sacrifice; he offered not gold or silver, or a whole world, but himself, more precious than millions of worlds composed only [i.e. even supposing they were composed only of] of angels and innumerable spirits as excellent as the omnipotence of God could create.

'[H]imself'. Not only his body of flesh, not only his soul a spirit, but himself, his whole person. His soul, his body, himself, the Son of God and the Son of man. He loved us as he loved himself, above what he loved himself, shall I say? He exposed his life for us, his most holy person for us. The act of his murderers is not regarded as a sweetsmelling savour, but his own act of obedience.

To whom did he thus give himself? '[T]o God'. To that God, to whom, by our base apostasy, we had rendered ourselves obnoxious and had fallen under his deserved wrath.

Our Saviour was God's before, as he was the Son of God, but he delivers himself to God as a Mediator, a victim to satisfy for our sins and reconcile us to our injured Creator. He offered himself to God as the judge and revenger of sin, the guardian of the law, the assertor of his truth in his threatening. He appeared before God as sitting upon a seat of justice, that he might open to us a throne of grace.

To what end did he deliver himself? '[A]n offering and a sacrifice'. Not [merely] *like* an offering, or [merely] *like* a sacrifice, but an offering, a sacrifice; not to do us a small kindness, but to offer his life for us. He was pleased to die in our stead that we might live by his death. He was not only an offering, but a sacrifice, an incense to be consumed into smoke, a sacrifice to be struck and bled to death. All the offerings and sacrifices of the law were completed in Christ. All his life wherein he acted for the glory of God was an offering. In his death, he bled and expired as a sacrifice; he underwent a death, not honourable, but ignominious, and not only ignominious among men, but joined with the legal curse of God. As he was the Son of God, he gave himself, having power to do it (John 10:18). Unless he had been the Son of God, he could not have been a sufficient sacrifice for us.

'[F]or a sweetsmelling savour'. He gave himself with an intention to be accepted, and God received him with a choice acceptation [acceptance]. Sacrifices under the law were accounted by God as a sweet savour (Exod. 29:41; Lev. 1:9; 3:16). This expression is first mentioned at the time of the sacrifice of Noah (Gen. 8:21). So God is said to smell an offering (1 Sam. 26:19). God accepted Noah's sacrifice, and took an occasion from it of declaring his counsel to Noah that he would not destroy the world, implying that he would in time recover it by the promised Seed. A [facility of] smell is here attributed to God. As good scents recreate and refresh the sense of a man, so did the sacrifice of Christ please and content God. Our sins had [would have] sent up an ill savour to heaven and had [would have] disturbed the rest of God. Christ expels our ill scent by the perfume of his blood and restores a sweet savour in the heavenly places, 'purified the heavenly things themselves' (Heb. 9:23).

God, being a pure Spirit, could not be taken with the smoke of the legal lambs nor refreshed with the fumes of incense; but both God and believers under the Old Testament had a content in them, as they were [in that they were] shadows of this sweet sacrifice which was intended for the appeasing [of] God and securing [of] the offending creature. What the legal sacrifices could not perform, as being earthy, mean and too low for the acceptation [acceptance] of God and [which] delighted him no otherwise than as they referred to Christ; this sweet sacrifice of the unblemished Lamb of God, possessed with a perfect love both to God's glory and man's safety, performed and sent up such a fragrance to the nostrils of God that he approved both of the priest and the sacrifice infinitely above the best sacrificers and sacrifices under the law. This sacrifice changed his countenance towards the filthy creature that had raised such noisome streams [unpleasant smells] in his presence.

We must notice these points: the love of Christ was the spring [mainspring] of his passion [sufferings]; the person of Christ was consecrated for us and given to us.

But the only things I shall take notice of are: (1) Christ was a voluntary sacrifice; (2) Christ was an efficacious sacrifice.

The sacrifice and sufferings of Christ for us were free and voluntary.

His offering was a free-will offering. It is expressed in the same chapter: '[He] gave himself for it [the church]' (Eph. 5:25). His voluntariness was typified by the paschal lamb, a lamb being the mildest of all creatures, resisting neither the shearers nor butchers (Isa. 53:7). All his work is assigned to his love (Rev. 1:5, 6). His love was antecedent [prior to] to his shedding his blood and our being washed in it. Love renders any work delightful. The Sun of righteousness has not a less bridegroom [-like] spirit and cheerful disposition in running his humble race than the sun in the heavens is expressed to have by the psalmist, in running his natural race in the heavens (Ps. 19:5). He was not made poor by force, but became so and laid aside his own riches for our sakes (2 Cor. 8:9). He became destitute of the advantages which other men enjoy, so that from his worldly poverty we might become rich in spiritual graces. He was not emptied of his glory by another, but he made himself of no reputation. He took upon him the form of a servant. It was not imposed upon him by constraint. He was not debased by others till he had humbled himself to the lowest degree of humility. He could have resisted them when they lifted him up upon the cross, but he wished to be obedient to the determination of his Father to the last gasp (Phil. 2:7, 8).

The hiding the majesty of God under the form of a servant, his descent not only to the earth – the lowest dregs of the world [universe], the footstool of the Divinity – but to the most abject and forlorn condition in that earth. His taking the similitude of weak flesh and running through all the degrees of reproaches and punishment, even to the grave itself, were voluntary acts, the workings of his love that he might rescue us from a deserved hell, to advance us to an undeserved heaven and make us partakers of that blessedness [which] he had voluntarily quitted[11] for our sakes. He willingly put himself into the condition of a servant, which is to be at the beck [beck and call] of another and have no will but that of his master's. He submitted his reason and affections to God, to be employed in his work according to his will. He had an absolute power over his own body (John 10:18), yet he made a free offer of it and subjected it to the penalty to be inflicted on him. Let us look at one more text: '[F]or their sakes I sanctify myself' (John 17:19). It cannot be meant of his consecration to his office of priesthood. That depended upon the call of his Father. He was constituted a priest, not by his own intrusion, but the Father's election, settled by an oath. The Father, and not [he] himself, glorified him in this regard (Heb. 5:4, 5). Again, this text cannot refer to his habitual and inward holiness, for he was sanctified by the Spirit at his conception and filled with all graces (Luke 1:35; John 3:34); but it is meant of his offering himself a sacrifice. His Father made him a priest; the Spirit made his human nature fit to be a sacrifice; his own will made him an actual offering.

In handling this doctrine, I shall do these four things: (1) Lay down some propositions for explaining this; (2) State the evidences of this voluntariness; (3) Show the necessity for it; (4) Make applications of the text.

Some propositions for explaining this.
(1) The Father's appointing him to be a sacrifice does not impair his own willingness in undertaking. The Father is

---

1   This is figuratively expressed. Christ, as to his divine nature, was always in heaven (John 3:13). Ed.

said to send him and deliver him (John 3:34; Rom. 8:32). This does not mean that the Son was over-persuaded, or came only out of obedience without any inclination of his own. The Father being the root and fountain of the Deity, all actions are originally ascribed to him, though common to all [three persons of the Godhead]. So he is first in order of being as he is first in order of working. The Father is said to deliver him, because the first motion of redemption is supposed [understood] to arise from the will and motion [action] of the Father; yet the love of Christ was the spring of all mediatorial actions and his taking our nature on him. Therefore he is no less said to give himself than the Father is said to give him to us and for us. God is said to set him forth (Rom. 3:25), yet he is said to come (Matt. 20:28). He was not thrust out, or forced to come. God lays our sins upon him, yet Christ is said to bear them. His engagement was an act of choice, liberty and affection. He could not be constrained by his Father to undertake it. His will was as free in consenting, as his Father was in proposing.

The Spirit is said to be sent by the Father and the Son to take of Christ's and show it to us, to fit those for heaven that [who] are given to Christ. Yet his distributions are according to his own will (1 Cor. 12:11) dividing to every man according as he will. If you consider Christ as one God with the Father, there is but one and the same will in both. Will belongs to essence or nature. The essence of God being one, there are not in God different wills, though the Godhead is in divers [different] persons, because the power of willing is the nature, not a person propriety. The decree of redemption was joint in Father and Son. What Christ decreed as God, he executed as man. And what he willed from eternity, he began in time to will as man. Christ, as God, gave himself to death with the same will and by the same action as the Father gave him. But as man, he gave himself by a will inspired by the Father. Yet for our understanding's sake, the scripture represents things as if they were distinct wills. But we must not imagine that there are really two wills in God. The scripture in condescension to our weakness represents God with eyes and ears and hands. But we must not conceive God to have a fleshly body like ours.

(2) The necessity of his death [does not] impeaches [detracts from] the voluntariness of it. Many things are voluntary, which are however necessary. There are voluntary necessities. God is necessarily, yet voluntarily, holy. The devils are necessarily, yet voluntarily evil. It is not in their power to become good, yet they are carried to evil with a complete will. Man desires to be happy by a natural and therefore necessary inclination, yet willingly and without constraint. Christ's death was necessary by the determination of God, yet also voluntary by a cheerful submission of Christ [on Christ's part]. The election of the good angels rendered their standing necessary, but the adherence of their wills to God made their standing also voluntary. Grace did not force them against their will, nor God's determination of Christ render him a sacrifice against his mind.

(a) It was voluntary in the foundation. The decree was not necessary, but [was] an act of divine liberty. Nothing can incline God to an act of grace, but his own most holy will. Christ being at liberty whether he would espouse our interest or not, his undertaking to manage it was a pure voluntary act, arising from his own will. He was not bound to become a creature or take upon him the form of a serv-ant, but his entering into that condition was an act of free

choice and condescension. No reason can possibly be supposed why the Son of God and Lord of the creation should
make himself lower than the angels for us, by any necessity
of his own condition. There was, indeed, a necessity for us
who could not be redeemed without him, but no necessity arising from the divine nature. If a creature ready to
be famished is in a place where there is only one person of
ability and sufficiency to relieve him, there is a necessity on
the part of the poor creature to be relieved, and relieved by
that person since there is no other to help him. But there
is no necessity on the part of the sufficient person to relieve
him. The help he affords him will be a mere act of charity.
This act of Christ is therefore called grace: '[T]he grace of
our Lord Jesus Christ, that, though he was rich, yet for your
sakes he became poor' (2 Cor. 8:9). Nothing could move
him to become either a creature or a servant in a created
state, but the yearnings of his own bowels [compassion]
towards fallen and miserable man.

(b) It was necessary after this engagement [i.e. Christ's
commitment to die for us]. His engagement to make
himself liable to punishment in our stead was free, but
when he had entered into bonds [obligation] to the Judge
of heaven and earth, he was then in his [God's] power
to be delivered up to death, according to that obligation
which he subscribed and consented to. He was then legally,
and by his own consent, bound to perform what he had
undertaken, and could not justly detract [withdraw]. The
promises of Christ are 'without repentance', as well as the
gifts of God. After Christ had put himself into the state
of a creature and form of a servant, the homage due from
a creature to God and the work of a servant after his ear
was bored was necessary, and could not be refused by him.

He had [would have] then broken his word passed to his Father in the covenant of redemption, had he absolutely declined it. 'He ought to die as Christ' (Luke 24:46) that is, as clothed with our nature for such an end. He needed not to die, as he was the Son of God by eternal generation and lay in the bosom of his Father; but it was necessary as he was made under the law, made Christ, that is, anointed to such a purpose. It was necessary also, in regard of the truth of God laid to pawn [pledged] in several promises, prophecies and legal representations. But still the fountain of all this was the free bubbling up of infinite affection to mankind.

Yet this necessity was a necessity of immutability, not of constraint. The holy and unchangeable will which complied with the first proposal remained in force till the final execution. The will of the eternal Spirit, whereby he offered himself to his Father, was immutable. It is a necessity arising from himself, and the perfection of his own nature; from his own holy will, not from any constraint. God cannot be constrained. Liberty is so essential a property of the divine nature that though it may determine itself, it cannot constrain itself. To be God is a term of infinite power; to be constrained is a term of impotency. These would be contradictions in the Godhead.

Besides, in his human nature he could not sin. He could not be overcome by the devil, who could find nothing in him as a foundation to stand upon (John 14:30). He could not do any thing against his Father. But to desert his suretyship had been [would have been] contrary to that law to which he had subjected himself. The word of the oath, whereby he was constituted a priest, had been [would have been] fruitless. It had been [would have been] the utter ruin of all the gracious decrees of God, because all the elect were 'chosen us in him' (Eph. 1:4, 5). The covenant with Abraham and the patriarchs had been [would have been] null, the oath which he sware to them, broken (Luke 1:73), and the foundation of their faith falling. The whole superstructure had been [would have been] dissolved, and they would have believed God in vain.

All this necessity is no plea against Christ's willingness. The obligation which the truth of God lays upon him, after he hath promised, does not diminish his first kindness and grace in making the promise. As the necessity of his death did not extenuate [minimise] the Jews' sin in butchering him, so neither doth it lessen Christ's willingness in laying down his life after he had voluntarily entered into our bonds.

(c) Though his death was violent in regard of man, yet this does not abate [diminish] the voluntariness in regard of himself. Judas betrayed him, the serjeants apprehended him, Pilate condemned him and the soldiers crucified him. But these were but instruments to execute the counsel of God (Acts 4:28). Yet he need not have been apprehended [arrested] unless he was willing. He showed his power to escape, not only [from] the united [combined] force of the Jewish nation, but of the whole world, by striking his apprehenders to the ground with the majesty of his looks. He that can rescue himself from the hands of men and will not, may be said to die willingly, though he dies violently. They slew him as murderers and made him a sacrifice to their revenge, not to God. This they did 'by wicked hands' (Acts 2:23) and with wicked minds too. He was the sole offerer of himself, as it respected God and advantaged us [benefited]. Judas willingly delivered him, Pilate with an imperfect will condemned him, the Jews delightfully [delightingly] reproached him. But the intention of none of them was to make him a sacrifice of redemption. It was for 'their sakes I sanctify myself' (John 17:19), but it was not for our sakes the Jews butchered him. Judas delivered him for the silver and Pilate condemned him to preserve his grandeur; but he delivered himself with an excessive affection for us. His murderers had no regard to the making [of] him an expiation for the sin of the world. His oblation to God as a sacrifice was an act purely of his own will at the very time of his death, not of his enemies' rage.

In this capacity his death was solely the fruit of his love and the hovering of his soul over the lost sons of Adam. It did not arise from a necessity of nature, but [from] the will of his mercy to us. He gave himself, and gave himself out of love (Gal. 2:20). Enemies did not give him, nature did not give him. The inward transports [delights] and affections of his soul, the actings of his choicest graces, whereby his offering was rendered acceptable to God, his murderers were not the cause of. They had not [would not have had] force enough to crucify him, had not a joy been set before him which made him endure the cross (Heb. 12:2), that is, the things wherein he rejoiced, [just] as those things are called our hope, which are the object of our hope. The joy of Christ, which made him despise the shame and ignominy of the cross, was the glorious good [which] he should procure by his suffering: the expiation of sin, reconciliation of God, the new creation of the world. For the producing and ripening [of] such fruits did he hang upon the tree. This gave him contentment and pleasure in the midst of his indignities and this was increased, not impaired, by the fury of his enemies. Though his death, in regard of men, was violent, yet, as the death of a sacrifice, it was wholly voluntary.

(d) When our Saviour seemed unwilling to [do] it in the time of his agony [i.e. in Gethsemane], he was then highly willing. This was when he prayed earnestly that the cup might pass from him, and begins, 'Father, save me from this hour' (John 12:27). The strugglings of innocent nature do both times [i.e. both in the time referred to in John 12:27 and, later, in Gethsemane] end not only in a gracious submission to the will of God, but in an ardent desire that the will and glory of God might have their full accomplishment. '[B]ut for this cause came I unto this hour. Father, glorify thy name.' He means: do thine own work, and finish every part of thy will in me, and what thou hast appointed me to undergo. The state Christ was in must needs admit of some shrinkings in his nature, encompassed with our infirmities. He saw the comfortable influences of God suspended [withdrawn], the indignation of God for our sins breaking out, the guilt of innumerable iniquities imputed to him, and the law with all its curses edged against him, and himself left to bear the weight of all this and conflict with a wrath no creature ever bore before. The apprehensions of all these meeting in a clear understanding could not but raise suitable passions of fear and trouble in his human nature. If he had not known the greatness of the punishment he was to endure for our redemption, he had [would not have] undertaken to ransom us from he knew not what. If he had not feared it, he had not been [would not have been] a sensible man [i.e. a man with normal human feelings]. If he had not trembled at it, he had not been [would not have been] an innocent man. Suitable affections to God in his carriage [attitude] towards us are the necessary duties of a creature. God is the object of fear in his justice which leads to punishment, which Christ then was to be subject to. It had not been [would not have been] consistent with that reverence which Christ always showed to God, [for him] not to be sensible of the sharpness of those punishments which were then providing [waiting] for him as a criminal substituted in our stead.

Though the person of our Saviour was but one, yet he had both two natures and two wills, a divine and a human. Otherwise he were not [would not be] God and man. If he had not a human soul, he were [would not be] not a man; and if he had not a human will, he had [would not have had] not a human soul. As he truly took our nature, so he took the laws of it, whereby it cannot love pain, but shun whatsoever it apprehends hurtful to it. As death was an evil against nature, he desires to decline it; as it was to be an atonement for sin and appeasing of wrath through the dignity of the sacrifice, he desires to undergo it. He regarded it as man and so had some reluctance to it; he regarded it as a man designed for such an end and therefore submitted to it. '[B]ut for this cause came I unto this hour'. As it was a dissolution of nature, a fruit of God's displeasure against sin, and should for a time exclude his soul and body from the fruition of the divine favour and glory, though the personal union[2] should not be dissolved, he startled at it. For the more Christ loved the sense of the divine love, which he enjoyed in his life, the more grievous would the apprehension [awareness] of the want [absence] thereof be.

But when he considered that he was united to that nature that he might suffer in it and lay it down as a sacrifice to

---

2   The union of the two natures in the One Person of Christ, technically called the Hypostatic Union. Ed.

that Justice which brandished a naked sword against man and that without it the world could not be freed from that misery which sin had hurled it into, he then put his neck under the cross. Similarly, a sick man considers a medicine bitter and dislikes it, but remembers the intention of the doctor and the beneficial qualities of the medicine, and so readily accepts it. Both the dislike and the acceptance are acts of the same will for different reasons. The dislike is an act of nature regarding it as distasteful, the acceptance is an act of reason regarding it as wholesome. Now, was not the will of Christ as Mediator as victorious in the issue over the reluctance as it had been in the capacity of a man desirous of the removal of the cup? The human will yields to the divine will and conforms itself, not only in a quiet posture, to the resolves [plan] of God, but in an ardent desire that his [God's] will might be performed. There was more of obedience in 'Thy will be done, not mine' and more of ardent affections in 'Father, glorify thyself' than there was of reluctancy in 'let this cup pass from me' or 'save me from this hour'. He disclaims the will of his human nature to perform the will of his Father's mercy.

Wherein this voluntariness of Christ's death appears.
(1) He willingly offered himself in the first counsel about redemption to stand in our stead. When our necks were upon the block, and the blow from justice was otherwise unavoidable, Christ steps in, diverts the blow from us to himself and declares himself willing to suffer what we had merited, that we might escape upon that suffering. The Father proposed it, the Son consented to it: the will of God is antecedent [prior] to the consent of Christ, 'I come ... to do thy will, O my God' (Ps.40:7, 8), which will was the will

of God for our sanctification through the 'offering of the body of Jesus Christ' (Heb. 10:10). Though he knew every thorn in the way he was to pass, the greatness of the wrath he was to undergo, yet his heart leaped into the Father's arms with a full and ready consent at the first overture. The Father proposed it not with more affection than the Son entertained it with delight, 'I delight to do thy will, O my God'. He was loathe to leave expressing it, 'I come'; that is not all, 'I delight to do thy will'; nor doth it rest there, 'thy law is within my heart': it is so settled that it cannot be rooted out but with the utter dissolution [destruction] of my heart. Thus in the volume, or the beginning of the book, it is written of him.

In the book of Genesis, in the first promise, the second person in the Trinity, who is supposed to [i.e. whom we believe] appear to our first parents after the Fall, represents himself [as] a suffering Saviour and testifies his own consent to the suffering he was to undergo as the seed of the woman by having his heel bruised by the serpent, and the victory he was to obtain by breaking the serpent's head. When the counsel was resolved upon, Christ is said to [be] 'Rejoicing in the habitable part of his earth' (Prov. 8:31). His consent was passed before the world was [existed]; it was a delight to him, because of the glory of God's grace, to be made illustrious in the sacrifice of himself. It cannot be meant of the first creation, for that is supposed, and there could be no exulting delight in that, since the defilement of it by sin presently succeeded the laying on [of] the top-stone. It is meant therefore of the restoration of the world, which was to be wrought by this wisdom of God. Some, to invalidate the Deity of Christ, understand by 'wisdom' in that book [of Proverbs] and chapter an intellectual habit, which is ridiculous. The antiquity of the wisdom here spoken of is before the mountains were settled and before there were any fountains abounding with water. The wisdom here described was present with God when he made the world. It was entirely familiar with him, there was such a familiarity between God and wisdom, as between a father and a son (v. 30). 'I was by him, as one brought up with him', and peculiarly the delight of God.

(2) The whole course of his life manifests this willingness. His will stood right to this point of the compass [i.e. never wavered] all his life. He never had any defect in his understanding, nor did his memory of what was appointed for him ever fail him. In the time of his life he frequently mentioned the tragedy to be acted upon him, the manner of his death by lifting up on the cross (John 3:14). And he who was intimately acquainted with the prophets knew every circumstance of his death predicted in them. Many enter the lists [encounter] with difficulties out of ignorance, but the willingness of our Saviour cannot be ascribed either to ignorance or forgetfulness. He knew long before that Judas was to betray him, before such a design entered into the heart of Judas (John 6:64), yet cashiered [dismissed] him not from his family. He foretold the hour of his death; his desires were strong for it, he was straitened till he was baptised with that bloody baptism (Luke 12:50). He had little ease in his own bowels, as though it were a kind of death to him not to be a sacrifice: and when Peter would have dissuaded him from suffering, he uses [speaks to] him as smartly as he would have done the devil: 'Get thee behind me, Satan' (Matt. 16:23), implying that in that speech he was the same enemy, by giving him the

same title. And the night before, he does solemnly oblige himself to suffer by his deed, as well as he had before by his word; he makes his testament in the institution of the supper and delivers his will into the hands of his disciples. His heart was bent to wade [set on wading] through it; he gave them his blood in the sacrament to show how freely he would pour it forth the following day in a sacrifice. The free distribution of his body to them represented the free offering up his body for them.

(3) At the time of his death, he manifested this voluntariness in his whole carriage [demeanour]. When the time drew near, he declined it not; he would enter Jerusalem with hosannas, as if, when he went to his death, he went to his triumph. And indeed it was so, for by that oblation [offering] of himself upon the cross, 'triumphing over ... principalities and powers' (Col. 2:15).

He went into the garden, which was as it were the bringing himself to the door of the tabernacle to be offered to God.

He had at the passover bidden Judas execute quickly his traitorous intention, and now quickens the high priests' dull officers to apprehend him, when he told them twice that he was the person they sought.

He summoned not one angel to take arms for his rescue, though he could have commanded legions to attend him; but as he had rebuked Peter before for dissuading him, he now rebukes him for defending him. He is moved thereto by an ardency of zeal to drink the cup: 'shall I not drink ... [of] the cup which my Father hath given me'? (John 18:11).

He would not court the protection of Herod by working a miracle to please his curiosity.

As he would have no relentings himself, so he would not endure them in others, and therefore dissuades the women from expressing their natural affection in a few tears (Luke 23:28).

His soul was not wrung and torn from him, but he rendered [gave up] his spirit into the hands of his Father, and cried with a loud voice before that last act. So he died not by a defect of strength, but by an ardency of will. He was more delighted with his sufferings for us than we can be with the greatest worldly pleasures and grandeur, and valued reproaches for us above the empire of the world. To conclude: his soul was not torn from him, but 'he hath poured [it] out' (Isa. 53:12), even that which was dearest to him, as a man doth water, freely and willingly out of the vessel. '[H]e hath poured out his soul unto death'; he ordered death to come and fetch it.

Why this voluntariness was necessary.

(1) *On the part of the sacrifice itself.*
He was above any obligation to that work [which] he so freely undertook for us. When he 'made himself of no reputation', it was a work of his charity, not of necessity; and he was bound in no other bonds, but those of his own love. Nor could he be overruled to any thing against his own consent; for, being God 'equal with God' (Phil. 2:6), he was subject to no law, nor could he be constrained to bend under the terms and penalties of it. Christ as the second person was not under a law any more than the Father; for he was 'in the form of God', that is, had the same essence with God.

Suppose [If] he had been incarnate without entering into any bonds [responsibilities] for us, though so far as he was man, he was bound actively to obey the precepts of the law, yet not bound to endure the penalties of the law, unless he had been a transgressor of the precept. He was to have [must needs have] obeyed it as a creature, but not suffer the curse unless he had been a guilty creature. But he was not only 'made under the law' as an innocent creature, but 'in the likeness of sinful flesh' (Rom. 8:3), as like as possible could be, sin only excepted. And therefore [he] observed those ceremonial precepts which concerned creatures [people], as sinful. He submitted to circumcision though he had no lust in his human nature to be cut off, and baptism though he had no stain to be washed away. And indeed, as he was not, so he could not be a transgressor, being secured by his conception from any original taint, and by the union of two natures in one Person from any actual spot. If he could possibly have been a transgressor, the salvation of the elect had been [would have been] by chance. Being a creature, of the seed of the woman, he may be supposed to be under the condition of the covenant of nature; yet not violating [i.e. if he did not violate] that covenant, he could not justly die for himself.

(2) *Necessary on the part of justice.*
The satisfaction for sin was to be made by death, because man upon his revolt from God was by the immutable law bound over to death. Man could not satisfy the law but by death, and so must have lain under the bonds of that death for ever, and no convenient way could be found for his rescue, unless some one, who was not obnoxious [liable] to that penalty by nature, should suffer in his stead that death which he owed.

Now, had it not been [would it not have been] an injustice to inflict a punishment upon a person purely innocent, and unwilling to render himself in the place of the criminal?

No man can be justly constrained to pay either a pecuniary [i.e. a fine] or criminal debt for another without his own consent, either actual at the time of paying or suffering, or legal, when, by entering into the same bonds, he hath made himself legally one person with the debtor or offender. Had not Christ voluntarily undertaken it, justice had been [would have been] wronged instead of being satisfied. It would on no account have been just to punish one that had not been guilty upon his own score [account], or by substitution. The satisfaction of justice in one kind had been [would have been] an injury to it in another. Even so, the will of Christ could not have saved us without his suffering, because, as the law had denounced death, justice was to be satisfied by death. Nor could the sufferings of Christ have saved us, without his will. For none can be an involuntary surety. Had he not consented to have our sins imputed to him, the punishment of our sins could not have been inflicted on him. To take from any [person] what is not due, and when they are unwilling to part with it, is an act of plunder.

(3) *Necessary in regard of acceptation [acceptance].*
Christ's consent was as necessary as God's order. Had Christ suffered for us without the consent of his Father, the Judge of the world, though his sufferings had been of infinite value, because of the dignity of his person, yet God had not been [would not have been] obliged to look upon us as concerned in him, nor count him to us, or for us [i.e. without Christ's willingness to act as our Saviour no benefit would have come to us]. And had not Christ consented that they [i.e. his own sufferings] should be for us, they could not justly have been accepted for us or applied to us. It had been [would have been] an alienating [of] the goods against the will of the

donor. As God's order makes his sacrifice capable of being satisfactory [efficient], so the consent of Christ makes it capable of being accepted for us, and applied to us. The heathens would not offer a beast that came struggling to the altar. But God, under the law, regarded not the reluctance of the sacrifice, but the free-will of the *offerer*, which was necessary to make the sacrifice a sweet savour.

How much more necessary is the voluntariness of that person who was to be both sacrifice and priest! Love belongs to the integrity of a sacrifice. A burnt body without charity is of no value (1 Cor. 13:3). The merit of his death depended not upon the act of dying, or the penal part in that death, but upon his willing obedience in it, in conjunction with the dignity of his person; and without this, his soul might have expired without being a sacrifice.

As the disobedience of Adam rendered the world obnoxious [liable] to wrath, so by the voluntary oblation of Christ, justification is conferred upon believers (Rom. 5:19). His love made his sacrifice a sweet-smelling savour. By the pouring out [of] his soul is our redemption wrought: 'he shall divide the spoil with the strong; because he hath poured out his soul unto death' (Isa. 53:12), or 'He shall partake of the spoil with the strong'. He shall take us as his own spoils, who were before the devil's prey, and restore to us that blessedness which the devil rifled [robbed] us of. We are restored, and he himself exalted, not merely because he died, but because he died willingly. We would have hoped in vain for the benefit of a forced redemption.

Application

(1) *The way of redemption by a sacrifice was necessary.* Why should Christ so willingly undertake this task, be a man of

sorrows or lay himself down into the grave, if the atonement of our sins could have been procured at an easier rate? He that made the world by a word would have redeemed us by a word if it had been consistent with his own honour. It is at least necessary for God's greater honour and man's surer benefit. The application of it to us must be as necessary as the oblation [offering] of it for us. Think not a few tears, the heat-drops of a natural repentance, can expiate those sins for which Christ thought the best blood in his heart so necessary to be shed.

(2) *The death of Christ for us was most just on the part of God.* What Christ did willingly submit to, God might justly charge upon him as a debt due. That man who will enter into bond to secure [oblige himself to pay] the debt to the creditor or satisfy for the criminal to the governor, may justly be sued upon default [failure] of payment by the one and arrested for default of appearance [failure to appear] by the other. What he promised may justly be demanded of him.

(3) *How wonderful was the love of Christ!* To accept so willingly of such hard conditions for us, and die so ignominiously upon the cross [which] we had deserved! He knew the burden of sin, he knew the terrors of hell. Yet he did not shrink from the imputation of the one or the sufferings of the other. It was not a willingness founded upon ignorance but upon a clear-sighted affection [love for his people]. He was willing to be reproached that we might be glorified; he would be like to us that we might be conformed to him; and took our human nature that we might in a sort [manner] partake of his divine.

O wonderful love! To open his breast to receive into his own heart the sharp edge of that sword which was directed against us! Had not his feet been well shod with love, he would soon have turned back and said [that] his way was impassable. A courtesy is enhanced by the greater ingrediency of the will [amount of willingness] in it. Our Saviour had a double will in this matter, the will of the divine and the will of his human nature, like two streams from distant parts meeting together in conjunction. Worse than devils are we, if we are not ravished [delighted] with so great an affection, which made him leave the heaven of his Father's presence[3] for a time, to pass through our hell in the dregs of the creation.

(4) *How willingly then should we part with our sins for Christ, and do our duty to him!* O that we could in our measures part as willingly with our lusts, as he did with his blood! He parted with his blood when he needed not [to do], and shall not we [part] with our sins when we ought to do so for our own safety as well as for his glory. Christ came to redeem us from the slavery of the devil and [to] strike off the chains of captivity. He that will [prefers to] remain in them, when Christ with so much pains and affection hath shed his blood to unloose them, prefers the devil and sin before a Saviour. He will find the affront [insult] to be aggravated [increased] by the Redeemer's voluntariness in suffering for his [the sinner's] liberty. How willingly should we obey him, who so willingly obeyed God for us! Christ did not let his enemies snatch away his life, but laid it down. So too, our duties should not be wrung from us, but should gently distil from us. The more will in sin, the blacker; the more will in obedience, the sweeter. It is in this we should imitate our great pattern.

---

3   See Note on P. 114. Ed.

Having despatched [dealt with] the first doctrine about the voluntariness of Christ's death from those words 'hath given himself', I proceed to speak of the acceptableness of it, from this latter clause of the verse. Allusion is made here to the perfume God commanded under the law (Exod. 30:34). The spices were to be pounded [crushed], and afterwards put into a censer to be dissolved into a sweet fume [smoke], in the Levitical service. Christ was bruised by his humiliation, to be rendered a sweet perfume to God.

The sacrifice of Christ was acceptable to God, and efficacious for men.

There was a complete satisfaction made to God, the supreme Judge [who had been] offended. It was a satisfaction pleasing to him and effectual to free the guilty party from the obligation to [suffer] the deserved punishment. Christ was white, in regard of his innocence; ruddy [red], in regard of his bloody passion. Both put together made him the 'chiefest among ten thousand' (Canticles 5:10). The efficacy of this sacrifice, in many fruits of it, is fully expressed: 'to finish the transgression, and to make an end of sins' (Dan. 9:24). The apostasy of Adam was checked, the idolatry of the Gentiles overthrown, the atonement of sin made which could not be [made] by the legal sacrifices. Righteousness pleasing to God, and therefore everlasting, [was] introduced; all the predictions of [about] him [were] fulfilled. Consequently he is anointed, that is, fully settled in all his offices and declared by that anointing to be a complete sacrifice and the Prince of our salvation.

The last words [which] our Saviour spoke upon the cross gave us an assurance of this. He saw and knew the work completely performed, and then gave up the ghost: 'When Jesus therefore had received the vinegar, he said, It is finished:

and he bowed his head, and gave up the ghost' (John 19:30). 'All the prophecies of what I was to do, are accomplished; I have nothing else now to do, to render my undertaking complete, but the bowing down my head, and sending out my last breath to my Father.' All the sacrifices of the law, the daily and anniversary sacrifices, were shadows and images of him, and fulfilled in their main design in and by him. It could not be otherwise than acceptable. For since there was no omission of any thing required of him, no commission of any thing forbidden to him. The whole law, both the mediatorial law and the law of nature, were within his heart. The whole law was answered by his life. He paid an obedience, not by measure, for he had received the Spirit not by measure, to prepare him to be a victim for our redemption. It was acceptable to God for us. This is the sense in which the apostle must be understood. It was a sweet savour to God for those persons and those ends [objectives] for which he gave himself. As it was a sacrifice intended and offered to God for us, so it was accepted as a sweet-smelling savour by God for those persons and ends [objectives].

In handling this doctrine, I shall: (1) Premise [lay down] two things for the explanation of it; (2) Prove it; (3) Apply it.

I shall premise [lay down] two things for the explanation of it.

(1) *God was not absolutely bound to accept it for us.* Though this sacrifice was infinitely valuable in itself, and had it been without a divine order might have been counted a testimony of affection to the honour of God and the good of the creature: yet God might have refused any acceptance of it for us. He might have rejected every sacrifice but [except] that of the offender. If we consider it simply in itself, without

any previous order, without any covenant struck between the Father and the Son concerning it, he was not obliged to have any respect to the apostate creature [human race], upon the account of it.

But after a covenant struck between them, wherein it was agreed that Christ should lay down his soul as a ransom and offer himself an unblemished sacrifice for the sons of men; and that he should see the travail of his soul and by his righteousness justify many after he had borne their iniquities in his own body on the tree (Isa. 53:10, 11); God could not but accept it, unless he could have found a spot in the offering and charged him with a non-performance of any article covenanted between them. If it were according to the tenor [terms] of the covenant of redemption, it could not be refused by God, being consequent to his decree and promise.

But if we consider it in itself, God was not bound to accept it for us, though he might have had a high esteem of it. For, according to the tenor of his law, he might have demanded a compensation from the person of the sinner and laid the punishment upon the person upon whom he found the guilt, and exacted the life of the sinner as a sacrifice for the sin. The acceptableness of this sacrifice was from itself, in regard of the dignity of the person, the infiniteness of the sacrifice. But the actual acceptance of it for us was from the covenant and agreement between them.

When a man offers to give a thousand pounds for that which is not worth a thousand pence, the sum is not only a valuable, but an over-valuable consideration [estimate] for that which is desired. But the acceptance of this sum from the other depends upon the will of the person whose property it is. The death of Christ was a sacrifice of a valuable consideration for the sin of the world and sufficient to expiate the greatest crimes both for number and weight. But the receiving of it upon such an account [for such a consideration] depended upon the will of the Lawgiver, whose authority was violated in the breach [breaking] of the law and who, as the only Judge, had passed sentence on the offending creatures, and had 'concluded them all in unbelief' (Rom. 11:32) and sentenced the whole world under condemnation (Rom. 3:19). It must be accepted by him. Otherwise it would not have been valid for us.

In regard, therefore, of the value of this sacrifice, all the beneficial fruits of it streaming upon the creature [i.e. believers] are in scripture ascribed to the death of Christ. But in regard of God's acceptance of it for us, they are ascribed to the grace of God – to the grace of God, as appointing and accepting; to the death of Christ, as procuring and purchasing. The grace of God gave a virtue to the mediation of Christ in regard of its application to us; but the death of Christ had a value in itself, whether it had been accepted for us or not, or ordered by God to be applied to us. And as God respects the agreement in the promise he makes to us, so Christ doth not enter any pleas in respect of the intrinsic worth of his blood, but makes this agreement the foundation of them: 'I have finished the work which thou gavest me to do' (John 17:4). The prevalency [effectiveness] of it for us depended upon God's order [i.e. covenant].

Indeed, had he not finished the work, he could not have challenged [pleaded for] the reward promised. There was to be merit on his part before a reward on God's. Yet the sufferings on his part may be conceived without any reward on God's part, if considered separate from this agreement and divine transaction between them. We must not understand this as though, if God had not been obliged to dignify Christ for his sufferings by the promise he had made him, he would not have rewarded those sufferings out of mere goodness; for since God in his own nature is infinitely good, he cannot but love holiness and affection to him, and testify his approbation of it by some retribution [reward].

(2) *As the acceptance of it depended upon the will of the Lawgiver and Ruler, so the acceptableness of it depended upon the will of the Redeemer.* The apostle therefore saith, 'He gave himself for us'. The sweetness of it depended upon the will of the donor, in concurrence [harmony] with the will of God. The more of will there is in any act of a creature's obedience, the more savoury [delightful] it is to the divine majesty to whom it is paid. His love both to God and us made his sacrifice a sweetsmelling savour. The merit of his death depended not upon his mere dying or upon the penal part in that death, but upon his willing obedience in it, in conjunction with the dignity of his person. Without this he might have breathed out his soul without being a victim. Had not Christ's will been full and firm in it, that his sufferings should be for us, they could not justly have been accepted for us, or applied to us. It could not have been a payment of our debt, and the application of him to us had been [would have been] an alienating [of] the goods of another against the will of the proprietor [owner].

This sweet savour exhaled from [arose out of] his voluntariness. He was not dragged to his sufferings, but suffered more willingly than we had greedily sinned against God. We had conscience checking us in sinning, but Christ had no conscience checking him in suffering. It was his meat and drink to do his Father's will. As God's order makes his sacrifice capable of being satisfactory, so the free willingness of Christ makes it capable of being accepted for us, and applied to us. Involuntary services are rather passions [passive experiences] than actions. In them we rather suffer a service than perform it. There was obedience in every preparatory act of Christ, obedience in the last act, in suffering death. And it was his obedience in suffering, not simply the suffering itself, that made it meritorious of his mediatorial glory for us. 'Wherefore God also hath highly exalted him' (Phil. 2:8, 9), namely, because of his obedience to 'the death of the cross'. His joy in performing was the incentive of God's joy in valuing, accepting and rewarding it. God eyed his obedience in the crown [which] he gave [to] him. And it was in the consideration of his obedience in suffering that he advanced him to that excellent dignity.

That this sacrifice is acceptable to God and efficacious for us, will appear in several propositions [points of doctrine].

1. God took pleasure in the designment [design] and expectation of it.
(a) His eternal delights were in him, not only as his Son, but as a Redeemer. God's delight in Christ and Christ's rejoicing in the habitable parts of the earth, and delighting in the sons of men, are coupled together (Prov. 8:30, 31). God delighted in him because he delighted in the redemption of man. Hence God is introduced speaking with a kind of joy of this ransom, 'Then he is gracious unto him, and saith, Deliver him from going down to the pit: I have found a ransom' (Job 33:24) – that is, I have accepted a ransom,

and have a price in my hand. It is similar to the verse in Hosea: 'I am become rich, I have found me out substance' (Hosea 12:8); that is, 'I have got wealth enough'. 'So,' God says in effect, 'I have here price sufficient. Loose the chains of the prisoner.'

This finding is the same on God's part with acceptance, as finding on Christ's part is the same with obtaining, 'having obtained eternal redemption' (Heb. 9:12). It is the speech of God. Who else but the Ruler of the world and the Judge of all flesh has power to order the delivery of the captive? It is the exultation of his mercy at the appearance of a sufficient sacrifice for the forlorn sinner, whose soul was drawing near to the grave and his life to the destroyers. It is the triumph of mercy at the thoughts of it.

(b) What else was the ground of God's promises to Christ, but his pleasure in him for this undertaking? What else can be the meaning of those words, which the apostle cites to prove the Deity of Christ, 'And again, I will be to him a Father, and he shall be to me a Son' (Heb. 1:5). This means that God would be always to him a Father, accepting his obedience, and [that] he should always be a Son, offering upon the cross, or pleading upon the throne his sacrifice and sufferings. God is a Father to him as Mediator, to countenance, encourage, accept him, and all his undertakings. This is a promise made to Christ. What need [was there] of any promises to Christ, considered only as the Son of God equal with the Father? It is a promise to Christ as the seed of David for the place [passage which] the apostle cites it from is 2 Samuel 7:14. And if to him as the seed of David, it is made to him as Mediator, promising a kingdom to him upon his suffering, and an eternal acceptance of him as an obedient Son. The basis of this was his purging our sins by himself (Heb. 1:3). All the promises of God to Christ respect not Christ absolutely considered as the Son of God, but in the relation of [capacity as] Mediator, sacrifice, ransom for man. For they are all branches issuing upon [out of] that first promise to man in paradise concerning the Seed of the woman whose heel was to be bruised.

God promises to be a Father to Christ in the same sense that Christ owns [acknowledges] him to be his God and his Father after his resurrection (John 20:17). This respects God's relation to him as Mediator, for as he is considered absolutely as the Son of God, God could not so properly be said to be his God. The term implies a covenant between them, in pursuance of which Christ was to be God's servant, and in acceptance of this God was the God of Christ and promises to be his Father, manifesting his fatherly and gracious acceptance of his services, as a father does the obedience of a son. Therefore Christ pleads the righteousness of God for obtaining the accomplishment of his grace in those that believe in him, as well as the love which God bore to him as Mediator: 'O righteous Father', etc. (John 17:25, 26). Grace was the fountain of the promise, but justice is obliged for the performance.

(c) *Hence it was that he declared his acceptance of him at his entrance into his office, which was at his baptism*: 'This is my beloved Son, in whom I am well pleased' (Matt. 3:17); not respecting only his eternal filiation, but the work into which he was entering, and the preparations to his being a sacrifice. With this work, wherein his Son was to glorify him, was God well pleased. Christ's interposition as a victim for the salvation of many brethren was pleasing to God. The Hebrew word in Isaiah 42:1, whence this place is cited, is often used to express God's pleasure in and acceptance of sacrifices offered to him according to his will (as Job 33:26; Mal. 1:8); and here it refers to the whole work of Christ, as the whole work of redemption is called the good pleasure of God (Eph. 1:5). He confirms here, by his own testimony, what he had declared before by the angels in their hymn: 'good will toward men' (Luke 2:14). So certain was God that this sacrifice would answer all his ends, that he testifies himself well pleased with Christ, before the full performance of his work.

(d) *Hence it was that God delighted to bruise him, including the thoughts of it.* He foresaw what pleasure he should take in this, as I may say, aromatic sacrifice, after it was bruised and pounded (Isa. 53:10). Not that God did delight in the act of bruising, considered separately from the ends for which he bruised him, since all acts of justice are his strange works; but with an eye to the issue of it, which was the glory of his divine perfections, the recovery of lost man, the restoration of the health and soundness of the creation; as the physician delights not in the sharpness of the medicine he administers to the patient, or a surgeon in lancing the body, but as it conduceth to the health of the patient.

(e) *Hence it was that he took pleasure in the representations of it before it was actually offered.* Hence the very first service after the promise was probably a sacrifice [Gen. 3], as hath been said before; and the chief part of worship in the only church God had in the world for many ages consisted in sacrifices, the representations of this grand victim in the end of the world. In all those things, which could not upon their own account satisfy God, as not being suited to his justice and wisdom and not able to expiate the sin of a rational creature, he smelt a sweet savour, as they were images of this sacrifice, whence [from which] the greatest and most pleasant fragrancy [fragrance] should be exhaled [breathed out] (Gen. 8:20).

All this pleasure of God, [which was] testified before the oblation, was from the certainty of its accomplishment. God knew he 'laid help upon one that is mighty' (Ps. 89:19), mighty to please him, and give pleasure to us. God could not have rejoiced beforehand in that which should have come short of his expectation. It is inconsistent with the Deity [God] to have such a disappointment. The least failure in the sacrifice would have frustrated [disappointed] his contrivance [plan], and rendered it loathsome to God as the sin of Adam for which he suffered. But it was impossible for God to be disappointed, and impossible for the Redeemer, being God as well as man, to fail in the performance of his part. God could not come short of his satisfaction, or the sinner of his security.

2. God had a restoration of his rest, which had been disturbed by the entrance of sin, and therefore this sacrifice was highly acceptable to God.
He was God's 'servant ... in whom my [God's] soul delighteth', or had a rest (Isa. 42:1), excluding [in contrast or in comparison (?)] all other things from contributing to the rest or delight of God.

God rested in the works of creation as they were shadows of his wisdom, power and greatness; especially as they were outpourings of his goodness and answered [corresponded to] his glorious ends [intentions]. For the ground of his resting was a review of the goodness of them according to his own mind and idea. He saw himself and his attributes glittering [reflected] in the creatures.

But the rest of God was disturbed by the invasion sin made upon his rights in the world; and no sooner had he made the world and was 'refreshed' (Exod. 31:17), but [than] disorder and confusion, by means of sin, spread itself over that frame [i.e. the universe]. Because of this he cursed the earth, which he had newly made and gave sentence against man. And though it was tempered with the mercy of a gracious promise, yet he left him under some outward penal evils [punishments] all his days because of his revolt. God had no rest but in that Seed of the woman, whose heel was to be bruised by the serpent that the serpent's head might be shattered and bruised by him; and thereby an end put to that disorder which had entered by the serpent's breath [lies].

And therefore all the joy God has in his church, the best part of his creation, is from this rest or acquiescence [resting] in his love, or the object of his love: 'he will rest in his love, he will rejoice over thee ... with singing' (Zeph. 3:17).

Hence it is, that the temple, the type of Christ, is called, in regard of those shadows of him, namely, sacrifices daily performed in it, 'the house of my glory' (Isa. 60:7), 'A glorious high throne' (Jer. 17:12), 'the place of my rest' (Isa. 66:1). Could gold and silver, polished stones and artificial structures be the rest and throne of God? As little as the blood of bulls and goats could affect him of themselves with a fragrant smell. His sole acquiescence [pleasure] was in the temple of the body of Christ made fit to be a sacrifice, and represented by those types. Such a rest he had in him as a sacrifice, that upon that very account he gave all things into his hands. By eternal generation he had communicated to him the perfections of his [God's] nature. He was a mediatorial sacrifice and so God gave him authority to execute judgment, gave him a kingdom as large as his own, and seemed to veil his [God the Father's] own authority to increase his

[Christ's], and as it were stands behind the curtain. This our Mordecai, that saved us from death, manages all the concerns of his empire, and all to this end, that 'men should honour the Son, even as they honour the Father' (John 5:22, 23).

Such a perfect acquiescence [delight] hath God in him, that he will surely entertain nothing to the prejudice of the honour of Christ in his work. He will not have the best works and sacrifices of men to be partners and competitors with him. He will for ever discard all those that have not the same thoughts of him, the same satisfaction and glorious rest in him, according to their measures, as himself hath. No other sacrifice shall be of value with him for the atonement of sin, not a drachm [drop] of mercy, not so much as to the quantity of the cooling virtue of a drop of water, can reasonably be expected by those who refresh not themselves with that sacrifice wherein God found so delightful a rest. God has such a rest in this sacrifice, that it shall be the matter of the praises of the saints to all eternity in heaven.

3. The highest perfections of God's nature had a peculiar glory from this sacrifice.

All his perfections, not discovered before the sons of men, are glorified promptly, according to his intentions and resolves for their discovery. Not a tittle [tiny part] of his nature which was to be made known to the sons of men, but is unveiled in this sacrifice to their view, in a greater glory than the creatures [creation] were able to exhibit him. The 'knowledge of the glory of God [shines] in the face', or appearance, 'of Jesus Christ' (2 Cor. 4:6), that is, all the perfections of his nature are delineated in this saving sacrifice. In which respect some think that, of the 'fullness of the Godhead bodily' (Col. 2:9) is to be taken [understood], not only that the Deity dwelt in the human nature, but the full discovery of the perfections of the Godhead was in the appearance of Christ in his body as prepared for a sacrifice, as in a map and scheme, as clear as could possibly be represented to the view of men. It is in the purchase of our 'redemption through his blood' that he appears to be the 'image of the invisible God' as well as the 'firstborn' or head of 'every creature' (Col. 1:14, 15), the image of those perfections of the Godhead which otherwise had been [would have been] utterly invisible to man – the image, not of his will, as the Socinians[4] say, but of his nature.

Hence is the glory of the Lord, as well as the salvation of his people, the name and title of Christ, 'the glory of the LORD shall be revealed' (Isa. 40:5; Luke 2:32). His holiness was glorified in the discovery of the hellish filthiness of sin, his justice in the grievous punishment of it, his mercy to his creatures in giving the dearest thing he had a ransom for them. In him he appeared gracious as well as righteous, transcendently merciful in the exercise of the highest justice (Ps. 11:5). Both shone clearly in the head of this sacrifice, being tempered for the glory of God, and the good of the creature. The seat of Justice is turned into a throne of grace, puts on the quality of an advocate instead of that of an accuser, uttering absolutions [pardons] instead of condemnations. Since Justice is propitiated by the death of Christ, it steps in as agent in the justification of a believer (Rom. 3:25, 26). Justice, the main attribute to be dreaded by man, was so glorified and pleased by this sacrifice, that this alone would oblige him to forgive sin, if mercy should not have any suit for itself.

---

4   Followers of a heretic at the time of the Protestant Reformation. Ed.

4. Compare this sacrifice with the evil for which he was sacrificed, and which had invaded the rights of God, and the sweet savour of it will appear, as also the efficacy of it.

(a) This sacrifice was as honourable for God, as our sins had been a dishonour to him. As much glory accrued [came] to him by it, as injury was offered him by our sin. Our sin was the sin of a creature and the sacrifice was the act of that person by whom God made the world. The sin was the act of his creature-image, the sacrifice was the act of the 'express image of his person' (Heb. 1:2, 3). Sin was committed by man, and expiated by him who was God. It was not only a rational sacrifice for the sin of a rational creature, but a divine one.

The sin was an infinite offence in regard of the person against whom it was committed; the price was of an infinite value in regard of the person by whom it was paid. The dignity of the person makes a compensation for the malice of the crime; an infinite person was not more wronged by the transgression than he is righted by the dignity of the person who made the compensation for it. It is every way proportioned to the infinite guilt of the crimes for which it is offered and the infinite justice of God which was offended thereby. God had a price of a full value. He was fully repaired [recompensed] in his honour, and we [were] delivered from our chains.

In some respect the attributes of God were not so much dishonoured by the sin of Adam, as they were glorified by the death of Christ; Christ glorified by his sacrifice those perfections which were not then discovered nor discoverable to Adam in his innocence, [such] as patience and grace. This Christ did as well as [glorifying] those [attributes] which were particularly offended by the revolt of man. This sacrifice fully repairs the honour of God, which nothing else could do. The reason why the damned lie for ever under the weight of his wrath in hell is because by all their suffering they cannot restore that honour to God which they have robbed him of by their iniquities.

(b) Therefore a greater pleasure arose to God from this sacrifice, than noisomeness [offence] from our sin. The dignity of the person suffering was equal to the dignity of the person injured, and infinitely exceeding the quality of the person offending. The sin of a creature could never be so filthy, as the blood of the Son of God was holy. The noisomeness [offensiveness] of the first could not equal the sweetness of the latter. The stench of sin was not only balanced and tempered, but overpowered by the sweetness of this sacrifice. Divine justice was not more incensed [roused] against the crime than divine holiness was delighted with the offering. Sin was the sin of our human nature, the sacrifice was of the human nature in union with the divine, and offered up by an 'eternal Spirit' (Heb. 9:14).

The apostle in that text alludes to Genesis 8:21. God smelt so sweet a savour from Noah's sacrifice, the type of this, that he resolves never more to curse the ground or send a deluge upon the new world, though he knew [that] it would prove as bad as the old. For in the same breath, wherein [in which] God's resolution is discovered to us, his sense of the evil of men's imaginations from their youth is declared also. The fragrant odour of the one was above the noisome scent [foul smell] of the other.

Though our consciences are 'purged from dead works', which do morally pollute us as the touch of a dead body did ceremonially pollute the Israelite, yet they [i.e. our consciences] are but partially purged here to serve the living

God. There is not a service we offer, but hath something mixed with it contrary to the holiness of God; yet the evil fumes that steam up with our sacrifices of duty are over-powered by the rich perfume of the sacrifice of the Son of God. When for the foulness of our imperfections we deserve a repulse [i.e. God's rejection], yet for the sweet-ness of his sacrifice we find an acceptation [acceptance]. So much did the merit of his blood overcome the ill scent of our iniquities in the nostrils of God that he cancels our bonds [debts] which were due to him, and makes new ones of himself to Christ. He frees the creature from the deserved punishment and obligeth himself to give eternal life to every one that believes in him thus sacrificed, however noisome [loathsome] his sins wherewith he had affronted [insulted] heaven before.

(c) Therefore it is efficacious [successful] for man, because so pleasing and sweet to God. Sin did not so much hurt to the transgressor, as this sacrifice procures good to the believer. Sin took away spiritual life. Christ by his sacrifice procures a restoration of it in a fuller communication than before (John 10:10), a richer and more overflowing fountain than before, more abundantly than Adam in innocency who had it mutable [changeably] in his own hands, we immutable in the hands of our Head who is our life. We have it more abundantly than the patriarchs of the Old Testament who had it in hope, and we in the full exhibition. [We have] a spiritual life more firm than Adam's, ending in an eternal life more durable [long-lasting]. Therefore the grace of Christ surmounts the effects of Adam's sin. The apostle discourses of [on] the abundance of grace above the abundance of sin (Rom. 5:15-17). As Adam's sin barred paradise against him and his posterity, the blood of Christ, as oil to the lock, makes heaven's gates open easily for the re-admission of every believer.

5. His resurrection after his bloody sacrifice is a clear evidence of the sweetness of its savour with God, and its sufficiency for us. He was not totally swallowed up by divine justice, but surmounted all the strokes of it and lifted up his head above the waves that surrounded him. The fetters of death had not been [would not have been] unlocked, if his sacrifice had not been satisfactory. The justice of God might as well have discharged him without any sacrifice at all, as discharged him upon an insufficient one. The freedom therefore of the prisoner from his chains [i.e. Christ in his resurrection] is an evidence of the full satisfaction of the debt and the completeness of the sacrifice, since it is by that God whose name has that letter in it, 'by no means clear the guilty' (Exod. 34:7). The writ of execution was taken off: 'He was taken from prison and from judgment' (Isa. 53:8). By whom? By him who only had authority to release him, who became a God of peace by his sacrifice before he showed himself a God of power in his resurrection (Heb. 13:20). He was appeased as an offended Lawgiver, before he gave a judicial discharge as the supreme Governor, unloosed the chains of death, sent an angel as his officer to unlock the prison doors, the grave, and set him at full liberty, no more to be arrested. There could be in this case no forcible breaking of prison, he being in the hands of the Almighty God, who had as much power to keep him in the chains of death had his sacrifice been blemished, as he had to free him when his sacrifice was spotless. Justice therefore is fully satisfied, since the pains of death are unloosed (Acts 2:24,

25, etc.) for 'it was not possible that he should be holden of it', because the truth of God was engaged that his 'Holy One should not see corruption'.

This raising him was a justification of him; for when he was taken from prison, he was taken from judgment also, that no suits [accusations] could be brought against him or any new actions [charges] laid upon him. He was 'declared to be the Son of God' (Rom. 1:4), and if we take in verse 3, that seed of David also, which was prophesied of. And he was declared to be so with power, not only by the power that raised him, but by the power of the government of the world, wherein he was instated [installed] at his resurrection. For this act of God was a testimony that he had ordained Christ, and ordained him also to 'judge the world' (Acts 17:31). By this he was acquitted by God, as having done all that he did according to the articles [terms of the covenant] between them.

In that act all Christ's members have an original and fundamental discharge [from punishment] to be sued out [pleaded and won] in due time in particular upon their faith [i.e. when each of the elect comes to faith]. It is in this discharge he triumphs, as it was his justification before men and angels: 'He is near that justifieth me; who will contend with me?' (Isa. 50:8). This is the foundation of the apostle's triumphant challenge: 'O death, where is thy sting?' (1 Cor. 15:55, 56). Where is sin, that ushered death into the world, and by it stung man to the heart? It is conquered by the resurrection of Christ, which is a clear evidence of the sweetness of this sacrifice to God and its efficacy for [power to save] us. Our faith is not in vain, which it had been [would have been] , according to the apostle, 'if Christ be not raised' (1 Cor. 15:17), as he died, namely, in the quality of our Surety and Head. Had not the sacrifice been without exception, the devil had been [would have been] the victor, and Christ would have been Satan's triumph. He would have acquired a stronger power over men by the least blemish [in Christ's sacrifice], as he first gained by Adam's sin. Had Christ not been justified himself, he could never have justified us, nor could the mercies of David have been sure and perpetual without it (Acts 13:34). So mightily pleased was God with this sacrifice, that he employed his glorious power to raise him. Justice had no plea to continue him in prison nor the devil any power to hinder the breaking of his fetters. His sacrifice was his act to propitiate God; his resurrection was God's act to comfort us.

6. The ascension and full exaltation of Christ after his bloody sacrifice, is a full evidence of this doctrine.
Since the promises made to Christ are accomplished, which were conditional upon the making of his soul an offering for sin, it manifests [that] he is an unexceptionable [blameless] sacrifice. He had a kingdom promised him, and now rules in the majesty of God (Micah 5:4). Had there been the least blemish upon Christ, he could not have claimed the performance of any one promise, nor had justice been [would God's justice have been] bound to make any [promise] good to him. Grace to man made the first promise to Christ in favour of justice, and justice would have hindered the performance of any promise, had it been able to find any exception. This sacrifice of his, in pouring 'out his soul unto death', is the foundation of all his advancement (Isa. 53:11, 12). Since this was the condition on his part, it could only be followed, upon the fulfilling of it, with a performance of the promises on God's part. Now Christ went first to

heaven in his soul immediately after his oblation to present his sacrifice to God, and receive his judgment about the validity of it. For that day, the day of his sufferings, he was to be in paradise: 'after death the judgment'.

This was agreeable to the type of him in the anniversary sacrifice upon the day of expiation, when the high priest was to go with the blood into the holy place immediately after the shedding of it, and sprinkle it on the mercy-seat; for after the blood was clotted, it was incapable of being sprinkled. Christ immediately after his death appears in heaven to receive the acceptation [acceptance] of his Father. This was in his soul, his body then lying in the grave, which the scripture calls not an ascension till his soul and body were re-united, and both went up to heaven together. By this first entrance into heaven, Christ obtained eternal redemption for us. Had not this judgment passed from God, concerning the prevalency [success] of his sacrifice, God had never sent [would never have sent] an angel to unlock the grave nor a cloud as a chariot to carry him up to heaven. This supposes his sacrifice on earth to be already ratified in heaven. By this ascension he was again declared, as well as by his resurrection, to be without sin and without any need of repeating his sacrifice (Heb. 9:28). His triumphant entrance into heaven assures us that his sacrifice was admitted into the bosom of God with infinite delight and pleasure. Christ could not have had glory, if he had not punctually [precisely] observed his order [i.e. God's will]. Triumph does not precede, but follows a victory.

His going to the Father was a full conviction of the righteousness of his person and his punctual [complete] discharge of his office [as our Saviour]. The chief topic whereby the Spirit should argue men into a compliance with [faith in] him (John 16:9, 10) is, because he is gone to the Father. Heaven had been [would have been] no place for a blemished and imperfect offering. The angels had not been [would not have been] commanded to be his adorers but rather with their flaming swords would have chased him out of heaven. He could as little have continued there if he had had any blemish, as Adam in paradise after his transgression. No gift could have been poured out upon the sons of men. The Holy Spirit could never have been the purchase of an unaccepted sacrifice. He could not have been invested with a power to exercise any office in heaven, if he had not executed what he had undertaken upon earth. He could not have lived to apply his sacrifice to us, if he had not been accepted in his offering [of] himself [as] a sacrifice for us.

But, since he sits at the right hand of God, it is an infallible token of God's absolute rest in him, and his own rest from any further labour. It is an argument of special favour and dearness. God has given him all power in heaven and earth, ordered all the angels to worship him, and not only to give him a simple adoration, but to be at his command, his ministers and attendants in his kingdom; he subjected his whole court [of heaven] to him and his service. He bestowed upon him all the honour that was possible to be given him as Mediator, out of the complacency [delight which] he had in him as a sacrifice. It was upon the account that 'he purged our sins' by himself, that he 'sat down on the right hand of the Majesty on high', and had all that dignity conferred upon him which is afterwards named in passages such as Hebrews 1:3. The whole prophecy of it is called 'a song of loves' (Ps. 45: title). So highly pleasing is it to God that he will put every enemy under his feet that doth not agree with him, because of his pleasure and delight in Christ (Ps.110:1).

As therefore he has entered into heaven and sat down at the right hand of God, and has maintained the plea of his sacrifice for so many hundred years since he first entered his suit, it is a proof that the pleading [of] his death and the sight of his sacrificed body is not wearisome and distasteful to God. It is not like a carcase that God desires to be buried out of his sight. He joyfully hears the voice of his blood sounding in his ears to this moment. Well therefore might the apostle upon this account make so great a challenge to all: 'Who is he that condemneth? It is Christ that died, yea rather, that is risen again, who is even at the right hand of God, who also maketh intercession for us' (Rom. 8:33, 34). Christ by his death appeased the wrath of God; by his resurrection, he was acquitted by the justice of God; by his ascension, he took possession of his regal throne; by his sitting at the right hand of God, he prevalently [successfully] pleads his sacrifice for the ends [purpose] for which it was offered and by his Spirit applies his blood to those who believe in him.

7. The admirable virtue of this sacrifice evidences the sweetness of it in the account [reckoning] of God.
Christ's sacrifice had a virtue antecedent [prior] to the oblation [offering] of it, and after the oblation it hath a perpetual virtue.

(a) It had a virtue antecedent to the oblation of it. God upon the foresight of this sacrifice to be made in due time, did dispense [give] his pardon to those that rested upon this future sacrifice. He did not stay [delay] till the satisfaction should be made for the injury committed, but imparted it to men who hoped in the merit of the sacrifice before the oblation of it, and released the captive upon the single bond [promise] of Christ before the actual payment of the ransom. Upon his promise to be a sacrifice, believers under the Old Testament were saved by the merit of it, as well as those under the New. Abraham rejoiced to see his day, and was justified by faith in him. When he appeared, his design was to 'put away sin' (Heb. 9:25, 26). What sin? Not only sins committed while he was in the flesh, or sins committed after his ascension, but sins before, even those transgressions which the legal sacrifices from the time of their first institution were unable to expiate. Such sins, which the high priest entering into the holy place every year with the blood of animals was not able to wipe off and to make that perfect which the law could not (Heb. 7:19) and redeem from the 'transgressions that were under the first testament' (Heb. 9:15). As a head appointed by God, he saved men before his coming, as Adam, the first head, ruined men before their birth. It is not more efficacious now, nor will it be to eternity, than it was before; for he is the same in point of virtue yesterday, in the ages past, as he is today at present, and will be in ages to come (Heb. 13:8).

Whoever were accepted by God in their persons and services were accepted upon the account of the first-born or head of every creature. In him all the elect were chosen and in him they were all accepted (Eph. 1:4, 6). Faith was from the first ages of the world; the proper object of faith is God in the Redeemer, and he was considered by the patriarchs, only in that quality [capacity], in all their sacrifices. This is because God had changed the government after the Fall from God as Creator to God as Redeemer. Therefore as all his acts of government respected the Redeemer and the redemption, so all the services of men were to respect the

Redeemer promised. What God did to them was in the name of Christ, the angel of his covenant; and what they offered to God was with an eye to the promised Seed, which is the same thing as our doing all things in the name of Christ, the circumstance of time only being altered. What was future then has been changed into time past now. The ground of this was the agreement between God and Christ for the performance of this oblation. When bonds are agreed on, and time given for the payment of the debt, the prisoner hath his liberty till that revolution [moment] of time.

Now, not only the thing to be done, but the time when it was to be done was settled between them, called therefore a due time or a stated opportunity (Rom. 5:6), and the fullness of time; and till that time there was to be a relaxation or pretermission [overlooking of the debt for the time being], a not charging the debt upon them, which is the word used by the apostle: 'for the remission of sins that are past' (Rom. 3:25). Had not this sacrifice had a virtue antecedent [prior] to the oblation of it, Christ himself in the days of his flesh could not well have uttered those words so often, 'Thy faith hath saved thee', before he had bowed his head upon the cross. The removal of sin, the bar to communion with God, upon the credit of a future sacrifice, is an undeniable evidence how sweet the expectation of it was to God. And therefore sweet music the actual sacrifice of it must needs be.

(b) After the oblation it has a perpetual virtue. If the virtue of it, before it was offered, reached to the first ages of the world, as far as Adam and Abel, it will continue in as excellent a force to the last believer who shall close up the number of the elect at the end of the world. If the blood of Abel is so efficacious as to procure a perpetual vengeance

175

upon Cain, shall not the blood of that person by whom God created the world, be more efficacious to procure a perpetual blessing from [out of] the grace of God, to which he is more inclined than to acts of vengeance? Though this sacrifice was but once offered, yet it works in regard of its virtue perpetually as a moral cause. Just as, when the act of sin ceases, the guilt and power of sin remains binding over to punishment, so, though the act of Christ's offering himself ceased, yet the virtue of it is durable [ongoing]. The blood of this redeeming victim [i.e. Christ] is intimated to be an incorruptible blood: 'ye were not redeemed with corruptible things, as silver and gold ... But with the precious blood of Christ' (1 Pet. 1:18, 19). Precious because incorruptible; the opposition [contrast] testifies it, though it be not the same expression. Precious blood is opposed to corruptible things.

As his body, so likewise his blood, and the efficacy of his sacrifice, was not to see corruption; his blood is like the rod of Aaron, always flourishing in the holy of holies before the mercy-seat. Aaron's rod flourished after Aaron's death, the sacrifice of God is always freshly rising before the throne of God, producing the fruits it merited and the grace we want [need]. This blood is called 'a new and living way', as if it were just now shed or had been sprinkled upon us as soon as it streamed out of his body. Since he is a priest for ever, the virtue of his death abides for ever. He could not be a priest for ever without an everlasting sacrifice, for priest and sacrifice are correlatives. If he be a priest for ever, he is a sacrifice for ever. The same moment that the virtue of the latter ceaseth, the honour of the former would shrink away. But the priesthood is 'unchangeable' (Heb. 7:24). His kingdom cannot be shaken; his sacrifice therefore, which was the foundation of his kingdom, cannot be wasted. He must cease sitting up his throne, fall from being the Father's darling at his right hand, if the virtue of his merit and the efficacy of his blood should cease producing the true fruits of it among his people. Though the oblation [i.e. Cross] was but once, yet the presentation is perpetual; he pleads upon his throne what he offered upon the cross.

If it were a wasted thing, it were [would not be] not worthy of the plea of so great a person as the Redeemer, nor worthy to be pleaded before so great a person as the Judge of all the world. He is, in regard of the continued virtue, not said to have been, but to be, our propitiation: 'he is the propitiation for our sins' (1 John 2:2), he is, not has been, he is *now* sitting in heaven. He was a propitiation on earth in his offering; he is a propitiation in heaven in the presentation of that offering. While his plea is heard, his death is accepted, for his plea is only the voice of his blood and the fumes [smoke] of his sacrifice. If the gospel must be preached to the end of the world, the virtue of his sacrifice, upon which the efficacy of the gospel depends, shall endure as long as the world endures.

This perpetual virtue was typified by the ashes of the red heifer burnt without the camp, which were reserved for purifying from legal uncleanness (Num. 19:9). As the power of the devil shall never be able to pull him out of his throne, so the power of sin shall never be so prevalent as to weaken the virtue of his blood. As long as he remains in a state of life, his blood will have its efficacy because it is the blood of 'the everlasting covenant' (Heb. 13:20). What greater evidence can there be of the gratefulness of it to God, than its virtue reaching to the most distant ages of the world and running through all the revolutions of time?

8. It is so acceptable to God, that it is a sufficient sacrifice for all, if all would accept of it, and by a fixed faith plead it.

It is sufficient for the salvation of all sinners and the expiation of all sins. The wrath of God was so fully appeased by it, his justice so fully satisfied that there is no barrier to a re-admission into his favour and the enjoyment of the privileges purchased by it, but man's unbelief. The blood of Christ is a stream, whereof all men may drink, an ocean, wherein all men may bathe. It does not lack value to remove our sins, if we do not lack faith to embrace and plead it. As no sickness was strong enough against the battery of his powerful word when he was in the world, so no guilt is strong enough against the power of his blood, if the terms upon which it is offered by God are accepted by us. It is absolutely sufficient in itself, so that if every son of Adam, from Adam himself to the last man that shall issue from him by natural descent, should by faith sue out [ask God for] the benefit of it, it would be conferred upon them. God has no need to stretch his wisdom to contrive another price, nor Christ any need to re-assume the form of a servant to act the part of a bloody sacrifice any more. If any perished by the biting of the fiery serpent, it was not for want of a remedy in God's institution, but from wilfulness in themselves. The antitype answers to the type, and wants no more a sufficiency to procure a spiritual good than that to effect the cure of the body.

He is therefore called 'the Saviour of the world' (1 John 4:14). And when the apostle upon the citation of that in the prophet that 'whosoever believeth on him shall not be ashamed', concludes that there is 'no difference between Jew and Gentile', but that 'whosoever shall call upon the name of the Lord shall be saved' (Rom. 10:1, 13). By the same reasoning it may be concluded, that there is no difference between this and that man, if they believe. What is promised to one believer as a believer, is promised to all the world upon the same condition. And when the apostle says in verse 9, 'if thou shalt confess with thy mouth the Lord Jesus, and shalt believe in thine heart ... thou shalt be saved'; he speaks to every man that shall hear that sentence. If any man believe, this sacrifice is sufficient for his salvation: as Adam's disobedience was sufficient to ruin all his posterity descending from him by natural generation. So is this sacrifice sufficient to save all that are in Christ by a spiritual implantation. The apostle's comparison would not else be valid: 'as by the offence of one judgment came upon all men to condemnation; even so by the righteousness of one the free gift came upon all men unto justification of life' (Rom. 5:18).

And if all men in the world were united to him by faith, there could not be any more required of Christ for their salvation than what he has already acted; for it is a sacrifice of infinite value, and [what is] infinite knows no limits. Since it was sufficient to satisfy an infinite justice, it is sufficient to save an inexpressible number; and the virtue of it in saving one argues a virtue in it to save all upon the same condition. Who will question the ability of an almighty power to raise all men from death to life, when it has raised one man from death to life by the speaking of a word? If men therefore perish, it is not for want of value or virtue or acceptableness in this sacrifice, but for want of answering the terms upon which the enjoyment of the benefits of it is proposed. If a man will shut his eyes against the light of the sun, it argues an obstinacy in the person, not any defect in the sun itself.

9. The effects of this sacrifice show the acceptableness of it to God.
As the effect of Adam's disobedience demonstrates the
blackness and strength of his sin, so the fruit of this sacrifice evidences the efficacy of it. Had it not been sweet
to God, we had still been [should still have been] in our
sins. He was to perfect his people, which had been [would
have been] impossible had he not been perfect himself in
his sufferings. If he has 'perfected for ever them that are
sanctified', then that sacrifice whereby he did perfect them
is fully complete (Heb. 10:14).

(a) *Remission of sin.* Our lives by our rebellion were a debt
to the violated law. When we transgressed the precept, we
incurred the penalty. This debt is discharged to believers
by Christ's offering his soul in their stead, a sacrifice for
sin, a rescue for their souls. He 'taketh away the sin of the
world' (John 1:29) – as a sacrificed lamb. The analogy relates
not to a lamb as a creature, but a lamb as a sacrifice. He
took away the sin of the world, the guilt of sin, the curse
of God. Whatsoever belongs to the eternal wages of sin,
he transferred upon himself. There is a perpetual virtue in
its nature: 'He taketh'; as when we say a drug purges, we
signify not only the act, but the natural quality of it. The
apostle concludes the efficacy of this oblation from God's
remembering sin no more: 'their sins and iniquities will
I remember no more. Now where remission of these is, there
is no more offering for sin' (Heb. 10:16-18). The completeness of the fruit discovers [reveals] the judgment of God,
for [in view of] the completeness of the merit upon which
it is founded. He himself therefore after his resurrection
gives his apostolic commission to publish this as the fruit
of his death, to let men know that the way to heaven in the

removal of the barrier was secured by the blood of Jesus (John 20:22, 23; Luke 24:47).

All the sacrifices wherein there was a daily remembrance of sin were abrogated as useless after this offering, which surmounted the efficacy of all the legal ones put together. They expiated ceremonial uncleanness and the pollution of the body; this [the sacrifice of Christ], moral iniquities and the filth of the soul (Heb. 9:13, 14), the apostle instances in the most solemn offering, that of the red heifer, supposed to be of a more durable efficacy than the daily offerings, since the ashes of it were reserved for 'a purification for sin' (Num. 19:9). But this, much more the rest, were exceeded by this offering that purged the conscience from those dead works that bound the soul over to eternal death. And indeed the ceremonial act of the high priest in sprinkling the blood of the heifer directly 'before the tabernacle' (verse 4), intimated that the efficacy of it was to be derived from the flesh and blood of Christ typified by that structure [i.e. tabernacle]. By this we gain a plenary indulgence [full pardon], so as to have 'no more conscience of sins' (Heb. 10:2). Not that there is no more sin in believers or no more sense of sin, but no more accusations and charges of sin before God or despairing servile thoughts for sin in their own consciences. For in his blood 'we have redemption ... the forgiveness of sins' (Eph. 1:7).

Upon this account a challenge is made by the apostle to all the believer's adversaries to bring an effectual charge against them (Rom. 8:33, 34). It frees us not from one or two sins, but vast numbers of them: 'the blood of Jesus Christ his Son cleanseth us from all sin' (1 John 1:7). So that all the powers of hell can never lay the load upon them again; for this saves to the uttermost, covers their iniquities and blots them out as a thick cloud. 'Death is swallowed up in victory', the destruction and condemnation by sin: 'O death, where is thy sting?' That is, where is sin; that is, the sting of death (1 Cor. 15:54, 55).

And indeed so acceptable to God was the first undertaking of our Saviour, that God promised him this as the fruit of his suffering that his labour should not be in vain, that he should see his seed, that by his knowledge he should justify many, when he 'bear their iniquities' (Isa. 53:11). And therefore when the apostle says, the old man is crucified with Christ, he understands that the destruction of the body of death, and the remission of all the extravagancies of it, is purchased by Christ at the hands of God (Rom. 6:6). And all the sense we have of remission, from any ordinance, especially by that of the supper, is not from the ordinance itself or the remembrance of this sacrifice, but from the perpetual and prevailing efficacy of it with God to this day. The removal of so great a weight from the soul which we were unable to bear, so great a curse which we were unable to suffer, shows the high acceptableness of it with God.

(b) *The confirmation of the covenant.* After sin had stepped into the world and invaded the rights of God, the first covenant became utterly unprofitable for the relief of man. God makes a new one, which was not signified to be valid to any without sacrifice. It is not unlikely that the first declaration of it to Adam, in the promise of the Seed, was accompanied with the sacrifices of beasts: both to show to him a token of that punishment [which] he had merited at the hands of justice and in what a bloody way his recovery was to be accomplished. The repetition of it to Abraham was confirmed by sacrifices (Gen. 15:17, 18). And the solemn covenant between God and the Israelites was confirmed by the sacrifices, and the blood of them called by Moses, 'the blood of the covenant' (Exod. 24:5-8), that is, a type of that blood which shall be shed for the confirmation of that blessed covenant whereby the soul shall be purified from sin. And by the institution of God this seems to be essential to a covenant with God: 'My saints ... that have made a covenant with me by sacrifice' (Ps. 50:5). And this custom was used by the heathens in their leagues and solemn contracts between nations, and in covenants between their gods and them, which descended [came down] to them probably by tradition from the first parents, though they had lost the true intent of that tradition. All this respected the confirmation of the covenant of grace (succeeding in the room of that violated covenant of works) by the blood of the promised Seed, whereby man was to be repaired [saved] and the devil defeated.

Hence is God so mightily affected with the engagement [commitment] of Christ to be our surety, that he presently establishes the covenant of being their God and making them his people: 'who is this that engaged his heart to approach unto me? saith the LORD. And ye shall be my people, and I will be your God' (Jer. 30:21, 22). That is the immediate issue of this engagement [commitment]. To this purpose was he given to be a witness of the everlasting covenant (Isa. 55:3, 4). And to this his sacrifice had an immediate respect, whence the blood that merits the striking off the chains of the prisoners and taking away the bars, is called the 'blood of thy covenant' (Zech. 9:11). And Christ, in the institution of the supper (Luke 22:20), calls it the 'new testament in my blood', that is, the true blood shed for the ratification of the covenant, which was only typified by the blood of all former sacrifices – and 'for the remission of sins'. This only is mentioned, though other benefits besides this flowed from the covenant, because as sin was the foundation of all evil, so pardon of sin is the fountain of all good. Had other blessings been merited without this, a barrier [would] had been put to our enjoyment of them, by the want [absence] of this. Upon this first link all other blessings in the chain of happiness depend.

All the promises of God, which are branches of this federal [coventantal] engagement, are 'yea and amen in Christ', of an infallible certainty. He himself is 'the Amen, the faithful and true Witness' (Rev. 3:4). And to this purpose is the sacrament of the supper appointed, being the perpetual representation of this sacrifice wherein God shows himself resolved to stand firm in the covenant which was confirmed by the blood of the cross, and make good to a believer all the branches [parts] of it. This manifests it to be highly acceptable to God, since the covenant made just after the unprofitableness of the old [covenant] is upon the account of this sacrifice ratified by God (as the sure mercies of David) in all the parts of it, to [supply] all the needs and [ensure] highest satisfaction of every believer.

(c) *Restoration of peace, and intercourse [fellowship] with God.* Man was upon the terms of enmity with God, hating him and being hated by him. God hates men, not as creatures, but as sinners. Man hates God, not as God, but as Sovereign and Judge. Man turned off [turned away from] God from being his Lord; God turned off [turned away from] man from being his favourite. Therefore Christ, in respect of this sacrifice, is called our propitiation (1 John 2:2; Rom. 3:25), alluding both to the sacrifices and the place of the sprinkling the blood. '[H]e was bruised for our iniquities: the chastisement of our peace was upon him' (Isa. 53:5). And though he was reconciling us all his life, yet it is principally ascribed to his sacrifice in his death (Col. 1:21, 22). All that Christ did in his life, had not been [would not have been] available for us, had he not added the top-stone in the shedding his blood. And therefore in the [Apostles'] Creed there is a transition and leap from his birth to his death, all intermediate actions of his life being omitted, because that was the great work whereby it was finished. Access to God was barred up, till the way was opened by the blessed Son of God (Heb. 10:19, 20). So much is God pleased with it that his majesty condescends [stoops] to the lowest step, to solicit [invite and plead with] his apostate creatures; and miserable man is admitted to importune God, not only with hopes, but assurance of his favour, and a happy success upon the account of this expiatory sacrifice. God hath laid aside the rigours of his justice, to beseech us with the bowels of his mercy, and tore down the partition-wall that hindered his deplorable creature from an access to him. He hereby has given us a full evidence of what an inestimable fragrance ascended from this sacrifice before him, since he did not only blot our sins out of the records of his justice, but restored us to his forfeited favour and conferred upon us the privilege of children and conversed with man as an object of his love, even though man before had rendered himself the mark [object] of his wrath.

(d) *The mission of the Spirit.* God first sent Christ to be an acceptable sacrifice to him, and to testify his high valuation of it, sent the Spirit in his name, or upon his account, to be an abiding Comforter to us. Had not the sin which first drove the Spirit out of the world, been expiated according to the mind and will of God, he had not [would not have] revisited the world, but left it in its original darkness. His first mission, and all his consequent operations, are the fruits of this sacrifice. Though he was sent by the Father, yet he was sent 'in my name' (John 14:26), as a fruit of God's acceptance of him.

His name had been [would have been] of no prevalence [advantage] for so great a gift, had not his death been first of a grateful savour with the Father. Had he not gone away, the Comforter could not have come to us (John 16:7). This refers not only to his ascension, but to his passion; and had he gone, and his death been disapproved of, the Spirit had stayed [would have remained] in heaven. Nor would the Spirit have been employed to bring things to our remembrance, which were not worth our remembrance to our comfort, if they had not been first worthy of his Father's acceptance. He was 'not [to] speak of himself' (John 16:13), that is, he was not to publish a new doctrine, but impress what Christ as a Prophet had taught, and what Christ as a Priest had acted. He would not have been sent to act upon a weak foundation and to propagate that which had not exactly answered [corresponded to] the will and design of God. He was to glorify Christ (verse 14), that is, to declare the efficacy of his death. Christ had not been [would not have been] a fit subject to be glorified in the world, had he not, in the administration of his office, glorified God, and been glorious in his eyes. And since he is an abiding Spirit, his perpetual inhabitation manifests the perpetual favour of this sacrifice; for, since the first acceptance of it was the cause of his coming, the perpetual fragrance of it must be the ground of his abiding. He could no more abide if there were an interruption of its sweetness, than he could first have come had there been a defect of sweetness in it.

This sacrifice did not only procure the coming of the Spirit, but his coming with the most glorious things in the possession of God: 'All things that the Father hath are mine: therefore said I, that he shall take of mine, and shall shew it unto you' (John 16:15). All things that the Father hath, the greatness of the Comforter, the fullness of the treasure, and his perpetual abiding with these rich gifts, are full evidences how much God is pleased with this offering. As God could not testify his good will to man in a higher manner than [by] sending his Son to be a sacrifice for him, so he could not in a higher manner testify his delight in that sacrifice than by sending so great a person as the Holy Ghost to be a solicitor to men to accept of it and a Comforter to those who believe in it. The third person in the blessed Trinity preserves the honour of the oblation of the second. God would never have been at the expense of so great a gift to keep up the credit of a person and sacrifice if he had no pleasure in him.

(e) *The acceptance of our persons and services.* His delight in this sacrifice is the ground of the acceptance of every person accepted by him. It is in the Beloved that every one is accepted (Eph. 1:6). [He is] not beloved simply as his Son, the second person in the glorious Trinity, but beloved as a sacrifice; for he was beloved as he was a medium for the praise of the glory of the grace of God, which was not as he was a Son by eternal generation, but as he assumed our nature by his incarnation, and offered it to God by his passion. The Trinity had been [would have been] blessed, if man had not been created, and had been [would have been] blessed, if revolted man had not been redeemed and not a spark of grace shot out upon the world. Therefore in the following verse, this, as well as the other parts of redemption, is ascribed to his blood.

Had not Christ been first accepted as an oblation of infinite value, neither the persons nor services of men, abounding with guilt and filth, could have been worthy of the notice and entertainment [favour] of God. Our acceptance is the fruit of the acceptance of the offering [which] Christ made of himself. The pleasure [which] God takes in his obedience to death makes believers as his members, and their services as sprinkled with his blood, delightful to God. For this reason, the last time wherein this victim was to be offered is called 'the acceptable year of the LORD, and the day of vengeance of our God' (Isa. 61:2), an acceptable time, when it was the day of vengeance upon sin in the suffering of the sinner's Surety.

(f) *The joys and peace of conscience.* By his bonds [promises] Christ procured our liberty; by his condemnation our absolution; and tasted of the vengeance of God to fill us with the delights of the Spirit. As God had a rest in his acceptance of it, so he gives us a joy and peace in our believing it, which is the acceptance on our part answering to the acceptance on God's part (Rom. 15:13). This is accompanied with a repose [rest] to the conscience, a silencing [of] our fears, and a filling with a 'joy unspeakable and full of glory'. These gifts God does most plentifully distribute [to] when we are deepest in sufferings for the acknowledgment and approbation [acknowledgement] of this sacrifice. It is then [that] Stephen shall see the heavens opened, and behold Christ at the right hand of God, have a sense [of] how highly God values that in heaven, which wicked men reproach, and believers suffer for on earth (Acts 7:55). Then it is that a 'spirit of glory and of God resteth upon you' (1 Pet. 4:14).

God eats not his morsels alone [i.e. shares his delight in Christ's Cross with us]. He impresseth a joy in the hearts of his people, when they are either publicly witnessing to this blood or privately acting [exercising] faith in it or celebrating the memorials of it. When we eat our spiritual meat with singleness of heart, God does accompany it with 'gladness' (Acts 2:46). Every beam of paradise, darting into the heart at such seasons, is a token of its sweet savour with God and an assurance of God's valuing us, for valuing that which is so much the object of his delight. Man only stands in a posture [position of eligibility] for such spiritual food when he is in the exercise of an estimation of Christ in imitation of that esteem [which] God has of him. This is the best savour to God, next to that of the oblation of his Son.

(g) *Bestowing the glory of heaven for this reason.* The restoring [of] men to that eternal salvation [which] they had lost is a certain proof of the strength of this sacrifice. As soon as Christ was 'made perfect, he became the author of eternal salvation unto all them that obey him' (Heb. 5:9). Nothing can be a higher demonstration to the sense of the creature of God's esteem of this victim than his admission of poor creatures to reside with him, for ever to behold and enjoy his glory. By this we have liberty to enter into the holy place, not only a licence or bare permission, but a right of purchase, whence it is called a 'purchased possession' (Eph. 1:14), a right of donation as a fruit of his delight in Christ, 'the gift of God is eternal life through Jesus Christ' (Rom. 6:23). Justice, that barred heaven, is satisfied; and God consented to a preparation of mansions in paradise instead of dungeons in hell, that his enemies might become the heirs of his kingdom. So agreeable to God is the odour of this sacrifice that God is not only content to free us from the hell we had merited, but he would [is willing to] also open for us the heaven [which] we had forfeited, that we might be partakers of the glory and kingdom of his Son: not only deliver us, but perfect us. He is ready, not only cross [i.e. cancel] our debts that entitled us to prison but [to] impute a righteousness to entitle us to glory. God is ready to stop the mouth of hell and open the gates of heaven.

Hence we are said to be raised together with Christ, namely, by the glory of the Father, as he was, to 'sit together in heavenly places in Christ', by the donation [gift] of the Father, as he did (Eph. 2:5, 6). The meaning of this is that by those acts of raising up and exalting to glory his sacrificed Son, he hath sealed to every believer the perfection of regeneration in a possession of glory for ever. The satisfaction God [which] has in the value of this offering, cannot give forth itself in fuller expressions than in our salvation by the virtue of it. Every thing formidable is and burdensome [fearsome] removed, every thing great and glorious bestowed, justice with all its vengeance appeased, the law with all its retinue of curses silenced, sin with all its demerits expiated, the covenant with all its benefits ratified, peace with all its blessings restored, the Spirit with all his treasures bestowed. Our services are purified from their filth, our consciences pacified from their fears, whatsoever is grievous abrogated, the veil of the temple with all the heavy weight of ceremonies rent in twain. Hell quenched, and heaven prepared and furnished for all who imitate God in his valuation of this sacrifice [i.e. who love Christ's Cross].

What was it that rendered this sacrifice acceptable to God and efficacious for us?

1: *The dignity of his person.*

That which is inferior cannot be the rest and satisfaction of a superior nature; nothing but infinite therefore can be the rest and satisfaction of an infinite Being. The holiness and goodness of any or of all creatures could not render a sacrifice worthy of the acceptance of God. The holiness of a creature was not infinite to answer the infinite evil of sin and suit the infinite holiness of God, any more than the weakness of a creature could have rendered him strong enough to endure the strokes [punishments] of an infinite justice.

Since the heavens are not pure in the sight of God and the angels, if compared with him, are not free from vanity (Job 15:15; 4:18), it is necessary that he in whom God rests should excel not only the dignity and perfections of angels but the condition of any finite being. If the holy angels cannot be the rest of God because of their natural mutability [changeableness] abstracted from [apart from] the establishing grace of God, much less can man who is filthy and drinks iniquity like water. For whatsoever dignity might be considered in his person to commend the sacrifice, might be considered also in his crime to aggravate the guilt. But the dignity of this person [Christ] was solely to be regarded in the offering, because he had no crime to be magnified by the consideration of it, being offered not for any sin of his own, but for the sins of others. This sacrifice was of infinite value, and therefore worthy of the acceptance of an infinite nature; his person was of as great a dignity as the Father's, to whom he was offered.

Though there be a distinction of order between the three Persons, yet not of dignity. He had no peer [equal] but God, for he was 'equal with him', had equalities of perfections with God, was in every way equal to the party offended, so that he is called God's 'fellow', one of the same nature with him: a man as stricken by the sword, yet his fellow as considered in his divine nature (Zech. 13:7). This is meant of Christ, part of the verse being applied by Christ to himself (Matt. 26:31) Christ is God's fellow, though man, yet not as man in whom the 'fulness of the Godhead bodily' (Col. 2:9), not typically as in the sanctuary and most holy place, nor mystically as in believers, but personally, as his flesh was the proper flesh of the second person.[5]

Hence that name which is peculiar to the essence of God is ascribed to him: 'he shall be called, THE LORD OUR RIGHTEOUSNESS' (Jer. 23:6). Jehovah, the incommunicable name of God, he, that righteous Branch whom Jehovah should raise up (verse 5) shall be called Jehovah. He that is raised up is Jehovah, as well as he that raised him; the glorious name of God would not have been ascribed to a simple [mere] man. He was in the form of God, before he took upon him the form of a servant, and laid not aside the form of God when he made himself of no reputation, and in that disreputed state became obedient to the death of the cross. Upon this account, his sacrifice is more worthy of acceptance than the sacrifice of all creatures. As the mediation of a prince is far more noble than that of a peasant, and the head of a king of greater value than that of a subject, the person of one David was more worth than ten thousand of the common Israelites (2 Sam. 18:3). And

---

5   This is a difficult sentence and has perplexed the editor. Ed.

as the person of Christ, so the sufferings of that person are of more worth than the souls of all men and their bodies cast into the scale.

The dignity of Christ thus appearing, let us see how his sufferings are dignified by the greatness of his person.

(a) *His sufferings were partly finite, partly infinite.* They were finite in regard of the time of duration; finite in regard of the immediate subject wherein he suffered, his human nature, which as a creature could no more become infinite than it could become omnipotent, omniscient or eternal. But in regard of the person who suffered, the sufferings were infinite, the Deity being in conjunction with the humanity. That which is finite in regard of time and in regard of the subject may be infinite in regard of the object. As the sin of a short minute, and the sin of a finite creature, in regard both of the time when it is committed and the person guilty of it, is finite; but in regard of the object, God, whose glory is eclipsed, it is an infinite evil. The greatness of an offence is to be measured by the greatness of the person whose honour is invaded. To hit a king is a capital offence; to hit an ordinary man falls under a small fine. So the value of a satisfaction is to be measured by the excellency of the person satisfying.

As therefore an infinite sin deserves an infinite punishment, because it is committed against an infinite God; so the sacrifice of Christ deserves an infinite acceptance, because it is offered by an infinite person. The subject sacrificed makes the sacrifice infinitely grateful [acceptable]. In the same way the person offended renders the injury infinitely heinous. This was not the sacrifice of a man or an angel; but of the head of the creation, 'the brightness of God's glory, and the express image of his person' (Heb. 1:3). By this circumstance his sufferings were advanced into infinity and the merit of them an infinite odour before God.

There could not have been so much honour rendered to God by the obedience of a mere creature, as there was injury offered him by the transgression of the sinner. Though our sins were not infinite in number, because no number can increase so vastly as to be actually infinite, since it is composed of units added to one another; yet had they been far less, they had [would have] needed an infinite virtue in the sacrifice by reason of the infiniteness of their guilt, because the majesty of God and his perfections are infinite, and these dishonoured by sin. This sacrifice has an infinite virtue of expiating.

(b) *This infiniteness arises from the near [close] and straight union of the divine with the human nature.* It was not the simple offering a sacrifice by the Son of God which was so acceptable. Had the Son of God offered any thing else, though the offerer had been infinite, yet the offering had [would have] been finite, because not allied to, and in conjunction with, the person offering. It was infinitely valuable, not because he himself was the offerer, but because he was the offering, offering that which was in conjunction with his deity [i.e. his human nature]. Purged by himself (Heb. 1:3; 9:14). By the personal union, the dignity was conferred upon the sufferings of his human nature.

If you say: 'A sacrifice would have been infinite, only because it was offered by an infinite person'. You may as well call the meanest worm in the world infinite because it was made by an infinite God and in an infinite manner of operation. The dignity therefore arises from the unity of the same infinite person, in whom the two natures were united. So all the actions of Christ, as Mediator, received their value from his person. And by reason of the unity of his person, that which was the act of one nature is attributed to the other: as when it is said, 'the Son of man which is in heaven' (John 3:13), that is, that person who was man though his human nature had not been in heaven. Also when his blood is called 'the blood of Jesus Christ his Son' (1 John 1:7) and the 'his own blood' (Acts 20:28); it was not the blood of the Godhead, but of that person who was God.

(c) In regard of this near conjunction, *the Godhead of Christ influenced every mediatorial action.* (I do not take in all the actions of the human nature, which had no respect to his mediation, any more than as they did refer to the sustentation [support] of his human nature, as his eating, drinking, sleeping, etc.) This value was as inseparable from his sufferings, as the divine nature was inseparable from the human. In all that he did, he was the Son of God: as much upon the cross, as before his descent from heaven; in the lowest pitch of his humiliation as well as in his highest state of exaltation; the Son of God as much when at his death he said, 'It is finished', as after his resurrection when he said, 'All power is given to me'. The man against whom the sword did awake, was 'my [God's] fellow', when he felt the piercing edge of it (Zech. 13:7).

Indeed, he laid aside the manifestation of his glory, but could not lay aside his glory; for then he might lay aside his eternity, omnipotency, his Deity, and cease from being God. This is utterly impossible. He was always the same and, as his years, so neither did his glory fail (Heb. 1:12). In all his sufferings he retained the relation and reality of the Son of God. The union of his natures remained firm in all his passions. Therefore the efficacy of the Deity mingled itself with every groan in his agony, every pang and cry upon the cross, as well as with the blood which was shed. And as his blood was the 'his own blood' (Acts 20:28), so his groans were the groans of God, his pangs were the pangs of God, and were therefore subjectively infinite in value.

Yet did not every groan and pang procure our redemption by itself, upon the account of the infiniteness of its value in being the groans of God, because they without death did not answer the tenor of the law; nor was the curse of the law, which he was designed to endure, accomplished in any act of suffering, without shedding of blood, and that to death: 'without shedding of blood is no remission' (Heb. 9:22). For as there was a necessity for the conjunction of the divine nature with the human, to make his sufferings infinite; so there was a necessity for a full conformity to the threatening of the law, and his Father's order, to make them efficacious for the honour of God and redemption of the creature. The sum is this: as what the divine nature acted [i.e. performed] was wrought instrumentally by the human; so what the human nature acted or suffered was made efficacious and dignified by the divine.

(d) *In this respect God, his Deity, may be accounted as it were his suffering, or as if he suffered.* It was not necessary that his deity should suffer to make the sacrifice infinite, and indeed it was impossible. The divine nature is as impassible as it is immutable; yet in regard of the straight union of the two natures, his mediatorial actions and sufferings, being the actions and sufferings of the person, may be counted as the sufferings of the Deity itself in a moral way, and by legal estimation. So sin is called Deicide [God-killing], not that it is so or can be so physically, but in a moral way in men's doing that which puts on the nature of destroying God, were it in the power of the sinner, or possible in itself. Similarly sin in scripture is called a wearying of God, when omnipotence cannot be tired, and if God were tired, he were not [would not be] omnipotent. But such people behave in such a way towards God that would weary the most patient man in the world. This is esteemed by God a wearying of him.

As Christ was not guilty of sin but in a juridical [legal] manner, by reason of his voluntary subjection to punishment in the stead of the sinner; so neither could the divine nature suffer but [except] by way of estimation, as the person of the Son of God did voluntarily assume the human nature wherein [in which] he was to suffer. Christ hung upon the cross as if he were guilty. The divine nature in conjunction with it might be esteemed to suffer, as if it were passible [capable of suffering]. The Deity did suffer in an eclipse of its glory, and veiling the manifestation of it. Hence, as he had a body, his blood was the blood of a man, yet because it was the blood of his person, it was the 'blood of Jesus Christ his Son' (1 John 1:7) and the 'his own blood' (Acts 20:28). The immediate subject suffering was the human nature, but the person suffering was 'the Lord of glory' (1 Cor. 2:8).

In that state and condition he offered up himself, which the apostle signifies: 'who through the eternal Spirit offered himself' (Heb. 9:14). '[T]hrough' imports not only that the divine nature of Christ did offer the sacrifice, but it seems to have the same sense as the same word: 'the father of all them that believe, though they be not circumcised' (Rom. 4:11).

The father of them that believe through uncircumcision, that is, in an uncircumcised state, or 'who by the letter and circumcision dost transgress the law' (Rom. 2:27). Not that circumcision was the cause of the one's faith, or uncircumcision the cause of the other transgressed, in those several states. So Christ here, when he offered himself, was not in the condition of a mere man, but had a divine and eternal nature in offering himself up to God. It is from this state and condition of his in his suffering that the apostle draws an argument for the value of his suffering above those of the legal sacrifices, and their excellence to purge the conscience, and puts the emphasis of a 'How much more' (Heb. 9:14). The very foundation of our redemption by his blood is his being the image of the invisible God: 'In whom we have redemption through his blood ... Who is the image of the invisible God' (Col. 1:14, 15).

(e) *Hence it follows, that the sufferings of this person, because of his dignity, were equivalent to an endless duration of punishment.* For the infiniteness of the person did more than recompense the shortness of the duration of his punishment. As the dignity of his person did outweigh the persons of all the angels and all men in the world, had they been without spot; so the time of his sufferings, though the moments of enduring them had been fewer, in regard of his greatness was equivalent to the eternity of the sufferings of all creatures. For it was more that God should suffer one minute than that all creatures in heaven and earth should endure torments to an endless eternity.

(f) *Hence it follows, that in regard to the dignity of his person, he was not only equivalent but superior to all those for whom he was a sacrifice; and to all, for which he was a sacrifice.* The sacrifice was as noble as the sin was vile, and offered by a hand more honourable than the person by whom the crime was committed could be unworthy. The dignity of the person was greater than the meanness of the offender could be base. The sin could not be more infinitely evil than the person satisfying was infinitely excellent. What an infinite object suffered by the offence was made up by an infinite subject expiating the crime. The dignity of his person is the reason why his righteousness has a sufficiency in it for all 'unto justification of life' (Rom. 5:19, 20). He is superior to all that were to be redeemed by him out of every kindred, and tongue, people, and nation, because he is 'God blessed for ever'. The oblation is greater than the offence, and the offerer than the transgressor.

What wrath so infinite that the blood of an infinite God cannot calm? What death so sharp and strong that the life of God cannot remove? It should be no less a cordial to us than it is a savour to God, to think that our sacrifice is as infinite as the wrath we had merited, and more infinite than the sin whereby we had deserved it. Our sin was objectively infinite, as committed against God. Our sacrifice was objectively infinite, as offered to God, proportionable to the honour he would have repaired, and subjectively infinite, in regard of the sacrifice offered for the reparation of it. God regarded him as the man his fellow, when he struck him; we should regard him in the same relation, when we plead him. To conclude: since this victim was equal with God, equal with him in essence, equal with him in nature and perfections, he could not be displeased with the sacrifice, unless he [i.e. God] had been displeased with himself, and his own nature.

As the dignity of the person, so the purity of the sacrifice, renders it fragrant to God, and efficacious for us.

His freedom from taint, and conjunction with the fullness of the Deity, are linked together in demonstrating the efficacy of it to purge our consciences from dead works: '[W]ho through the eternal Spirit offered himself without spot' (Heb. 9:14). He was as free from blemish, as [he was] full of an eternal Spirit. The spotlessness of his human nature was necessary to his being a sacrifice, and the union of the divine nature was necessary to his being a valuable one. As the legal lambs were to be without blemish, so was Christ a 'lamb ... without spot' (1 Pet. 1:19). He had no sin naturally imputed (juridically indeed he had), no sin personally inherent: he had no sin naturally imputed, because he was not in the loins of him [i.e. Adam] who introduced sin into the world and [who] derived it to his posterity.

His extraordinary conception by the Holy Ghost in the womb of the virgin was a bar against original sin; whence, by way of emphasis, as he is called 'that holy thing' (Luke 1:35). He was infinitely holy as he was God, habitually holy as he was man. Every faculty of his soul, every member of his body, was elevated to the highest degree of holiness. His human nature was holy by the union of the divine, holy by the effusion of the Spirit, whose office it is to sanctify. Though, by reason of the divine nature united, it was impossible for his human nature not to be holy (the person of the Son of God would never have assumed a tainted nature), yet the holiness of his human nature flowed from the stores of the Spirit, it being not the office of the second but of the third person to sanctify. But the human nature in conjunction with the divine could not but be pure. Had that been tainted while in union with the divine, making but one person, the taint might have been called the sin of God, as well as the blood of his body be called the blood of God. This is a thing therefore not imagined possible. He was holy in every action.

As he was man he was bound to all sorts [forms] of obedience; for, having taken the nature, he was subject to all the duties incumbent on that nature. He ran through every economy,[6] he observed the law of nature, conformed to the ceremonial part of the Mosaic institutions, submitted to the baptism of John, a middle state of the church, and therein 'fulfil all righteousness' (Matt. 3:15), the righteousness of the positive laws of God in every state. He was holy in all his offices, harmless as a priest, faithful as a prophet; holy in his life, holy in his death; no guile was found in his mouth, no inordination [excess] of murmuring in his heart.

Had there been any spot, which is impossible, his sacrifice could not have been for our sins, it must have been for his own. If his own debt could have been paid by it, ours could not. His spot had been [would have been] infinitely greater than ours can be. It had been [would have been] objectively infinite as ours, and subjectively infinite which is more than ours. The rights of God had been [would have been] more invaded, instead of being repaired. The guilt would have been as great in the sinner, as the satisfaction could have been in the sufferer, a subjective infiniteness in the sin, as well as a subjective infiniteness in the sacrifice.

But there was not, there could not, be any of this. Satan could not charge him with any, but confessed him holy (Mark 1:24). The all-discerning eye of God could see

---

6   Charnock means: Christ was obedient to God's will as made known in every prior period of history.

nothing contrary to his honour, but justified him as holy (Heb. 7:26). Impurity had been [would have been] contrary to the dignity of his person. God could as well be [i.e. could no more be] unholy, as the person of Christ unholy. His holiness therefore was infinite, though the holiness of his human nature was not of itself infinite, any more than his sufferings were of themselves, and in regard of the human nature, the subject suffering, infinite. Yet the holiness of his human nature derived an infiniteness from his person, as well as his sufferings derived from it an infinite value; so that there was an infinite holiness in this sacrifice offered to an infinitely holy God. It had no stain to be purged by the addition of another bloody offering. It answered the design of God, terminated the rest and delight of God. Such a holiness must needs then be highly acceptable to God who loves and is delighted with righteousness in his creature, and much more so with that of his only Son, the unstained and infinitely pure sacrifice [given] for us.

The graces exercised in this sacrifice rendered it fragrant in the account of God.

(1) *His obedience*

The acceptableness of it to God did not arise simply from his dying, but [from] his obedience in his death, 'became obedient unto death' (Phil. 2:8), and not only from an obedience to the law of nature, and the precepts of God as a creature, but his obedience to the law of redeeming love as a Mediator, and his delight in it (Ps. 40:8). As the disobedience of man shook the rest of God, so the obedience of the Son of Man settled the rest of the Deity. Obedience ran through the whole web of his life, he submitted to a body fitted for those dreadful strokes of wrath which we should have endured; a body made under the law (Gal. 4:4). He delighted in the thoughts of performing the will of God in our flesh; he came not to do his own will. Whatsoever the Father ordered him, that he spake, that he did, that he suffered. He laid down his body when the hour was come appointed by his Father.

It was not a simple but an affectionate obedience: 'I love the Father; and as the Father gave me commandment, even so I do' (John 14:31). Here principally his obedience to the mediatorial law is intended. Also he was 'obedient unto death, even the death of the cross' (Phil. 2:8) which the law did not oblige him to. The moral law bound over the sinner to death, but the mediatorial law bound over Christ to death in our stead. The obedience to the moral law, or law of nature as it concerned the state of angels, was performed by him without any defect. In this the obedience of Christ was greater than theirs, in regard of the infinite dignity of his person above all the angels in heaven. Yet the rule of their obedience was of the same nature. But in obedience to the mediatorial law, the Redeemer stood single [i.e. alone]; as he trod the wine-press alone, so in the whole mediatorial work none was in conjunction with him, none had any likeness or resemblance to him.

This was above the obedience of all creatures, not only in that it was the obedience of him who was God, but an obedience wherein he could not be imitated by any creature already created, or that could be created. For it was a work above the strength of any created being. It was obedience under the highest provocations to resume his glory, and come down from the cross, and declare at that moment the iniquity of those reproaches they cast upon him. It was obedience in the highest pitch of his sufferings, obedience in heaven, practising that compassionate obedience upon the throne which he 'learned ... by the things which he suffered' on the cross (Heb. 5:8), acting according to his Father's orders, presenting his obedience on the cross, as meritorious for his members [whom] he left in the world. If the obedience of Abraham, a sinful creature, in his willingness to offer up his son Isaac, a sinful creature also, was so pleasing to God, that thereupon he makes to him glorious promises; how much more grateful [i.e. pleasing] is the obedience of him who was God, and offered not up a son, but himself, a pure, not a spotted sacrifice. If obedience is better than sacrifice, then sacrifice is insignificant without obedience. Christ's offering himself a sacrifice according to the will of God for our sanctification was the most significant part of his obedience (Heb. 10:7, 10).

In this he did exactly answer [to] the mediatorial law as his rule, and God found the will of Christ in the performance fully conformable to his own will in the precept. He was more obedient to the will of God in his offering than Adam was disobedient to the will of God in his sinning. Such a height and perpetuity of obedience [was wonderful, considering that it was rendered] under all the circumstances of temptations, the strugglings of the flesh which could not but desire the removal of penal evil, under the fear of wrath also, the sense of agonies, and reproaches of men. In this way he testified, that he preferred the glory of his Father above the safety of his own nature, obedience to his command above the contentment of his flesh, and was swayed by the form of a servant to submit, against the suggestions of his nature as a man, to desire the passing [of] it away. All this, I say, rendered his sacrifice highly acceptable.

(2) *His humility*

His humility is joined with his obedience, as the cause of his exaltation, which was the evidence of its fragrance (Phil. 2:8). God loves to be imitated in his condescensions to his creature. The condescension of Christ [who was] equal with God, to the taking upon him the form of a servant, setting himself in the stead of the sinner, the eclipsing his own glory, shrouding it under the disguise of our flesh, submitting to a harder piece of service and a deeper humiliation than any creature in heaven or earth was capable of; to descend from heaven to earth, expose himself to the fury of men and devils without murmuring; to bow his head to the stroke, not of an honourable, but an infamous death, endure the wrath of a Father [whom] he loved, come down to the lowest step before he did re-assume the glory which was due to him, was an inexpressible and inimitable act of humility. Lower than this he could not humble himself. Since humility renders men so pleasing to God that he heaps upon them the greatest testimonies of his favour and richly dispenses to them the gifts of his grace (James 4:6), it must render the Son in those sufferings most acceptable to his Father and draw from him the greatest distribution of his favour, because it was the greatest act of humility, as well as obedience, that could possibly be performed.

(3) *His faith*

This resolution of trust he brought with him, and this resolution he kept: 'I will put my trust in him' (Heb. 2:13, cited out of Ps. 18:2). He had not a spark of infidelity [unbelief], or any grain of distrust in the goodness of God. He suffered for a time the torments of hell, without the despair of the inhabitants of hell; he had a working of faith under the sense of his Father's greatest displeasure and confided in his love while he felt the outward and inward force of his frowns. The sharpness of the scourge and the smart of his wounds beat not off his soul from a fast adherence to him.

He had a faith of the acceptableness of his death for his elect, and gave evidence of his confidence in the promise for a happy and glorious success, in acting like a king, while he was hanging as a malefactor on the cross, in distributing his generous gifts to the poor thief, assuring him that that day he should be with him in paradise. He let not his confidence in his Father flinch; he confided in him for the bestowing that royal power upon him, which he signified by this promise of paradise to this criminal upon the cross. And both his obedience to God in not turning away his back, and his trust in God for his assistance, are put together as the ground of his justification (Isa. 50:5, 7, 8).

The height of his faith was to be discovered in opposition to the unbelief of Adam; his humility, in opposition to the pride of Adam; his obedience in doing all according to God's order, in opposition to the disobedience of Adam. By his active and passive obedience, he glorified the holiness and justice of God; by his humility, the sovereignty and power of God; by his trust, the faithfulness and veracity of God: all which must needs render his sacrifice as a sweet-smelling savour, and efficacious for us.

In regard of the full compensation made to God by this sacrifice, and the equivalence of it to all the demands of God.

His obedience was fully answerable to the law, his active answered the preceptive part, and his passive the penalty. As he fulfilled the righteousness of the law in his life, so he underwent the threatenings of the law in his death. He obeyed the commands in our stead, and sustained the curse. He bore the sorrows [which] we should bear: 'Surely he hath borne our griefs, and carried our sorrows' (Isa. 53:4), spiritual as well as bodily. Our whole nature had sinned, and our whole nature must suffer; Christ took our nature that he might suffer what was due to our nature. He suffered in his soul which is the greatest part of our nature, as well as in his body which is but the case and sheath of the soul. It is against the order of justice for the principal [part, i.e. the soul] to sin and the accessory [i.e. the body] only to be punished. The punishment threatened against the first Adam was the death of the soul as well as of the body; the punishment borne by the second Adam was of the same nature; not a spiritual death, a separation from God by sin, that he was not capable of; but a moral death, a separation from God by desertion.

When he cried out, 'My God, my God, why hast thou forsaken me?' he was forsaken of God in regard of the sensible comforts of his presence, though not in regard of the invisible sustentations [supports] of his soul. The union of the two natures was not dissolved, but the comfort of the Father's presence was eclipsed. Though he did not suffer eternity of torments, yet he suffered what was due to us; for eternity of punishment is not primarily threatened in the law, but secondarily inferred.

Death was threatened, but because man cannot satisfy by death, therefore he lies under that death for ever. He is kept in prison, because he cannot pay the debt which was due, nor repair the honour of the law which was violated. Justice would always be striking, and never contented. If the honour of the law could have been vindicated and the justice of God satisfied by the temporary groans of a creature, not only the goodness of God but the justice of God would release him. But because the justice of God could never have been satisfied in this way, the person of the sinner must always have been [would always be] a sufferer. Christ therefore suffering a cursed death, suffered what we should have suffered; death was threatened to us, and death was inflicted on him; the eternity of death was accidental [i.e. not essential to make atonement].

As Christ obeyed the whole law, yet not every accidental relation of the law, as it respected men in particular states and particular callings and relations; as the duty of a parent to a child, of a husband to a wife; not for want of a principle of obedience in him, but for want of those particular relations to which those particular acts of obedience were annexed. So Christ suffered every part of the curse, but not the sins consequent upon that curse by reason of the corruption of man, nor the accidental continuance of the curse which the impotence of man to satisfy rendered him offensive to, but the strength of Christ exempted him from. He endured all that the law imposed upon sinners, whether in regard of loss by desertion, or in regard of sense by malediction. Hence he is said to be made a curse (Gal. 3:13) and to be made sin (2 Cor. 5:21).

And if so, he bore the punishment due to us, since the law threatened no more than a curse, and Christ bore the curse according to the threatening of the law. He suffered that which the law demanded of us, and was made such a curse as the law required. He suffered the torments of hell without the iniquities of hell, which were not possible to be committed by an infinitely holy person. He suffered those agonies which were of the nature of the torments of hell, and that desertion of God which is the sting of hell. Nothing was omitted that was demanded by divine holiness for keeping the commands, or by divine justice for violating the commands. As we were creatures, we owed God a debt of duty; as we were revolted creatures, we owed God a debt of punishment. Since our fall, sin has made us incapable of answer to the holiness of God in the performance of our duty, and our nature as creatures renders us too weak to satisfy the justice of God by enduring the penalty exacted by the law. Christ has done both and in answering the whole demand of the law, as to both debts, delights the holiness of God, satisfies the justice of God and by both repairs [saves] the creature [i.e. us].

If the creature could have satisfied justice for what was past, yet it still lay under a debt of duty for the time to come. If it had fallen short of this, it must have re-assumed its suffering. What a deplorable condition had this [would this have] been, to have come out of suffering one hour and to return to it the next! But our Redeemer performs an obedience that reaches to the utmost of the creature's duty, and endures a penalty that reaches to the utmost of the creature's demerits. A recompense was made by the obedience of Christ for the disobedience of Adam: '[A]s by one man's disobedience many were made sinners, so by the obedience of one shall many be made righteous' (Rom. 5:19). For what had the law to enjoin [require] which he did not perform, or what had the law to inflict which he did not endure? Had he not done and suffered what the law required, how could he be called the end or perfection 'of the law for righteousness' (Rom. 10:4)? Had he not suffered what was due to sin, he could not have made 'an end of sins'; and had he not done what the law commanded, he could not have brought in an 'everlasting righteousness' (Dan. 9:24). He is both a valuable price and sacrifice commensurate to the demerit of our crimes. He suffered whatsoever was requisite to discharge our debts, and could not have offered his soul instead of ours if he had not borne in his soul what we were to bear in ours. In regard therefore to the full compensation made to God, it must needs be fragrant to God and efficacious for us.

In regard of the glory Christ by his sacrifice brought to God.

The glory of God was that which he aimed at, and that which he perfected. It was the will of God which he came to do; but the design of God's will is to glorify himself, and declare his own name in all his acts. The glory of all the attributes of God appeared 'in the face', or manifestation, 'of Jesus Christ' (2 Cor. 4:6). They all centred in him, and shone forth from him in all their brightness, and in a full combination set off one another's lustre: not only in his incarnation, but also, and that chiefly, in his sacrifice. Mercy could not be glorified, unless justice had been satisfied; and justice had not been [would not have been] evident, if the tokens of divine wrath had not been upon him. Grace had not [would not have] sailed to us, but in the streams of his blood: 'without blood there is no remission'. Justice had not been [would not have] so fully known in the eternal groans of a world of creatures, nor could sin have appeared so odious to the holiness of God by eternal scars upon devils and men, as by the deluge of blood from the heart of this sacrifice. Wisdom in the contrivance had not been evident without the execution. The glory of the divine perfections had [would have] lain in the cabinet of the divine nature without the discovery of their full beams; and though they were active in designing it, yet they had not been declared to men or angels without the bringing [of] Christ to the altar. By the stroke upon his soul all the glories of God flashed out to the view of the creature. When Judas went out from his company to prepare the way for his oblation, 'Now', saith he, 'is the Son of man glorified, and God is glorified in him' (John 13:31).

The honour of God and the glory of the Son depended upon this point, and in this last act threw off all their veils. The Father was glorified in appointing him and the Son was glorified in submitting to be a sacrifice; the truth of God was glorified in bringing things to a period [i.e. fulfilment] and the obedience of his Son was glorified in his perseverance to the last act. His grace was elevated to the highest note in the songs of angels. An unsearchable depth of manifold wisdom was unfolded, a depth of wisdom more impossible to be comprehended in our minds than [if we had] the whole globe of heaven and earth in our hands. Such was the wisdom of God in the cross, which the angels never beheld in his face upon his throne: wisdom to cure a desperate disease by the death of the physician, to turn the greatest evil to the greatest glory, to bring forth mercy by the shedding of blood. The ultimate design of this victim was the honour of God in our redemption: 'I seek not mine own glory', but the glory of his Father (John 8:50) in the salvation of men. That which accomplished the triumph of all his attributes must needs be fragrant to God.

3. Uses of these doctrines

1. *If this sacrifice be acceptable to God, it is then a perfect oblation*. If it had not been perfect in itself, it could not have been accepted by an infinite justice, a justice inexorable

without it. An incomplete offering could have given but [only] an imperfect satisfaction, and that had been [would have been] as good as no satisfaction at all. God would never have approved it. An all-seeing wisdom could not be deceived, a severe justice could not have acquiesced in it, a pure holiness could not have smelt a sweet savour from it. God as a Judge delivered him to be a sacrifice, God as a Judge accepted him after he was offered; this sacrifice therefore answered the ends of God, both satisfied his justice, and glorified his holiness. How could God else [otherwise] judicially glorify him if he had not been fully glorified by him? If he had performed an imperfect obedience, he would at the best have had but a half exaltation, or rather none; but since he has been accepted with the highest pleasure, and has a glory in the highest pitch, he has performed an obedience to the utmost point, and touched the goal designed [for] him.

Though there was grace in God's appointing it, yet there was no grace given out to make it acceptable. God did not supply by his acceptance any defect in the sacrifice; there was a meritorious worthiness on Christ's part before there was an acceptance, but it was accepted because of its perfection. Infinite purity accepts nothing but what is perfect in itself, or has a relation to that which is perfect and agreeable to its nature. He does indeed accept the imperfect obedience of believers, but not for itself, but for this sacrifice, to which by faith it has a relation. Had it not had a gratefulness [merit] in itself, God could have scented nothing in it; he could not have smelt a savour where none was. It would have been as little pleasing to him as the burnt-offerings under the law.

This [sacrifice of Christ] could not but be perfect in the account of God, since there was the humanity in conjunction with the divinity to be the sacrifice, and the divinity in conjunction with the humanity to be the altar for the sanctification of it. And the sequel shows, that the offering has been as valuable as the offence was provoking, since in consideration of it, justice deals with the injuries done to the Deity and treats believers as heirs of heaven, instead of rebels. This is the inference the apostle draws from the priesthood of Christ (Heb. 8:12), and what is the fruit of his priesthood is the fruit likewise of his sacrifice. The righteousness of Christ is also perfect, since the all-searching eye of God sees nothing in it to give him any cause of distaste [i.e. to be disgusted]. It is perfect because everlasting (Dan. 9:24). All the righteousness of the holy angels in heaven, had there been numberless millions of them, had not been [would not have been] so pleasing to God as this.

2. *All popish doctrines of satisfactions, and all resting upon our own righteousness and inherent graces, are to be abandoned.* There is a natural popery in the minds of men. Fallen man is desirous to stand upon his own foundation, and is as little content with God's judgment of things as his first parent was in Paradise. We are studious of [naturally apt to] making God compensations, applauding ourselves in our own inventions and satisfactions of our own minting, unwilling to acquiesce in his wisdom.

(a) This is a high presumption. If Christ were a perfect sacrifice in the esteem of God, it is a boldness and blasphemy in us not to think him so. If it be perfect, what need of anything from us to piece it out? If it were not sufficient,

God was much mistaken to accept it; if it were not perfect, Christ had a lack of strength and holiness to be a sacrifice, and God a lack of wisdom to discern the defects of it. God was then deceived to count that sweet which needed something else to sweeten it. Such additions are an injury to Christ; it is to make him but half a sacrifice, since he hath 'offered himself without spot to God' (Heb. 9:14). Can we pretend to [have] any other, without charging him with weakness and deficiency? Is not his divinity enough to make his offering complete, without any supply from our corrupt humanity? Can we acknowledge that perfect, which we think needs something from us to strengthen it? It must be then a false assertion of the apostle, when he saith that 'by one offering he hath perfected for ever them that are sanctified' (Heb. 10:14). To make Christ in part a Saviour is to make him in part no Saviour, and to ascribe salvation to something else as well as to him.

All such satisfactions entrench upon [impinge on] the honour of Christ's sacrifice and pull the crown from his head to set it upon our own, or, at best, ascribe that in part to ourselves which is wholly due to him. By how much the more sufficient it is for us without any addition, so much the more glory redounds to the sacrifice. He needs no more of additions to sweeten his offering than he needed of cordials to strengthen and support him in the time of his sufferings. They are rather gall and vinegar offered him upon his throne, as the Jews did in the time of his oblation upon the cross. It is a high presumption in us not to be content to rest in that which is the rest and pleasure of God.

(b) It is a folly. It is as if a man should set up candles to increase the light of the sun, and eke out [intensify] its beams. Can the righteousness of a man add any perfection to the blood of God or perfect a work which could not be done by the Deity? If God stood not in need of any thing from us to perfect his work of creation, how can man be so foolish to imagine that Christ stands in need of any thing from us to perfect his work of redemption? If that sacrifice requires something to render it efficacious, it must be a sacrifice of the same kind. Nothing that is of an inferior nature can add an intrinsic value to that which is superior. What can man offer to God that can be in any sort equivalent to this sacrifice already accepted? All that we can offer to God is but as a few blasted ears of corn, such as Pharaoh saw in a dream, which can add nothing to the value of it. If there had been any failure in him, the defects of a Redeemer could not be repaired by the offerings of the captives. And if there is no failure, all additions and all other inventions to try to make atonement are superfluous.

How foolish will it be, to rest in that which God never pronounced or owned to be a sweet-smelling savour to him? If all our 'righteousnesses' be as a 'filthy rags' (Isa. 64:6) the offering of it up to God is a noisome stench [foul smell], not a pleasure. The best of our works and graces derive a sweetness and value from the virtue of this sacrifice, without contributing any thing to the savour [perfume] of it. It is a folly to leave a sure for an uncertain road. All other rests have no divine stamp and signature upon them. God never found any savour [perfume] in any other offering. The Spirit of God never gave any so noble a character as this, of a sweet-smelling savour, but as they had a relation to this as the antitype of them. This one victim sends forth more grateful odours [welcome fragrance] to God, and is more efficacious for the concerns of our souls than the joint intercessions of saints and angels.

Let us therefore be diligent in our duties, aim at the perfection of an inherent righteousness, but never place our confidence in them, or equal them to the sacrifice God hath so affectionately accepted. Did God ever set up his rest in the services of a creature? Can this be savoury [pleasing] to an infinite purity? Whatsoever is done without faith is but the offering of an enemy, whatsoever fair colours it may be outwardly adorned with. The scripture sets an impossibility upon the head of all these: '[W]ithout faith it is impossible to please him' (Heb. 11:6), to gain or keep his favour. Whatsoever is done without faith, though of the highest elevation, is but a creature, and therefore not the object of trust. And whatever significance believing works have, is from the tincture [dye] they receive from the blood of this sacrifice, wherein faith dips them, as being faith in the blood of Christ. Though Adam, while he continued in his created rectitude might have entered his righteousness as a plea; yet because it was mutable, it had been [would have been] no fit object of trust for him. But since our revolt [i.e. the Fall], all pleas of a fleshly corrupted righteousness are overruled in the court of heaven, and our pleas must run in another name [i.e. Christ's]; all other things have ceased to be savoury [pleasing] to God, since they were tainted by sin. Let men make 'the refuge of lies', and hide themselves under falsehood, the false coverings of their own righteousness, and think to shelter themselves from the 'overflowing scourge' (Isa. 28:15-17). It will be a miserable self-deceit, 'the hail shall sweep away the refuge', and the 'waters shall overflow the hiding-place'. All other hiding-places, but the smoke of this sacrifice, are too weak to preserve us from the overflowing waters of divine vengeance.

3. *It is a desperate thing to refuse this sacrifice, which is so sweet to God.*

(a) It is a great sin. As faith in Christ redounds to the honour of God, as being an approbation of his mercy, justice and wisdom, in the acceptance of this sacrifice; so unbelief redounds to the contempt of God, as slighting all the pleasure, the wisdom, the justice and holiness which God took in it, as though he were delighted with a sleeveless and unworthy matter [i.e. a trivial thing]. It is to trample upon that which is God's delight, accounting that which is sweet to the Deity loathsome to us, refusing to be guided by God's judgment of this offering, setting up our own wisdom, not only equal with, but above the wisdom of God. It is a regarding that which God is infinitely pleased with as a frivolous thing, as though God had pleased himself with a trifle [paltry thing], or smelt sweetness in a weed. God's acceptance of it owns [shows that there is] a fragrance in it; man's refusal calls it gall and vinegar, a rotten service. God's language is, 'This is my beloved Son, in whom I am well pleased' (Matt. 3:17); 'This is my fragrant sacrifice with which I am infinitely delighted.' The language of an unbeliever's heart is, 'This is an offering in which I can find no pleasure.'

The heart of God and the heart of an unbeliever, the wisdom of God and the judgment of an unbeliever, stand in direct opposition. How inexcusable a pride is it to think that not worth our receiving, which God has entertained [received] with the highest affection! To count that unsavoury, which God has accepted as the sweetest present that can be given him in heaven or earth! Unbelief cannot be excused without accusing God of weakness and folly. It is a sin against his precept, as he commands us to believe, a sin against his pattern, as he directs us by his own act to an acceptance of him. Other sins are against his sovereignty in the violations of his law. This is against his wisdom in his gracious acceptance of a propitiating sacrifice for us. We disown him as our Lord, and as our pattern.

(b) It will end in great misery. God will not suffer that which is sweet to him to be slighted by man without the recompense of a just indignation. The vagabond nation of the Jews[7] bears to this day the sad tokens of God's vengeance upon them, for the unworthy refusal of so great a victim. '[B]ecause of unbelief they were broken off' from the root (Rom. 11:20) and are deprived of all the sweetness which God and believers taste in it. Nothing in the world was ever the object of God's delight but this; nothing in the world can ever be pleasant to him without this. To neglect it is to neglect that which is the only thing God will accept, and so fall under the condemnation of law and gospel too. It is to reject God as a satisfied Judge, in the flowings of his mercy; to fall under God as a provoked Judge, in the thunders of his wrath. If we will not comply with divine justice in an estimation of it, we must fall under his fury for our contempt. If this offering be not cordially and upon God's terms accepted by us, we must be a sacrifice ourselves; Justice must have a sacrifice for every sinner, from himself or another. God in honour will not pardon sin without one, in greater honour he cannot but punish sin upon the

---

7   After A.D. 70 the Jews, as a judgment on their rejection of Christ, were scattered, like 'vagabonds' all over the earth till the setting up of the state of Israel in 1948, a date of course, far in the future for Stephen Charnock. 'Vagabond' is not meant as an insulting term here. Ed.

refusal of this. Oh how 'fearful a thing is it to fall into the hands of the living God!' a living, unpacified God, a living and reproached God, a living God who hath been counted a ridiculous fool by a wilful sinner, in his accounting the blood of the covenant as an unholy thing!

God will not have his wisdom justled [jostled] against by the folly of his creature. 'No other sacrifice remains for sin.' No other mark of distinction was appointed by God for the securing the first-born of the Israelites from the stroke intended for the Egyptian heirs, but the blood of the paschal lamb sprinkled upon the posts of the doors. Had any fed upon the lamb and neglected the sprinkling, he had [would have] felt the sharp sword of the destroying angel. The lamb had been [would have been] of no efficacy to him, not from any defect in itself, but negligence or contempt in the offender. The sacrifice of Christ has an infinite virtue to save. But it is no remedy to them that [those who] will not sprinkle their souls by faith with the blood of it. Without this, we shall remain in our unatoned sins, and have the sword of vengeance doubly whetted against us.

4. *It administers matter of comfort to the believer*. It is some comfort to all, that they are in a fair way of being happy. The justice of God was the bar to God and man's meeting together. It was morally impossible, in regard of God's truth and holiness, for man to be restored without a vindication of that law which had been broken. But now the honour of the law is restored by this sacrifice. God hath owned it, the bar is removed, and where God hath found a sweetness, man may find salvation, if he be not his own enemy, and wilfully cast away his own mercy. He 'gave himself a ransom for all' (1 Tim. 2:5, 6), a ransom in our stead, or

a counter-ransom, in opposition to the sin of Adam, the fountain of our bondage: for all, upon gospel-conditions. As he gave himself for all, so he was accepted for all upon the same conditions; for he was accepted as he gave himself. It is a comfort to a diseased hospital, that a physician is chosen and accepted by the governors, who is able to cure every disease. It is no less a comfort to a guilty soul that there is a sacrifice sufficient to expiate every sin.

But there is a ground of sensible comfort to those who believe. If when Christ walked upon the waters and was labouring in the floods of affliction in the days of his humiliation, he bid his disciples not to fear; how much more may we expel fear from our believing hearts, since he is sat down upon his throne and the whole merit of his sacrifice graciously accepted? Let us represent to ourselves this crucified, but now crowned victim, lying in the bosom of his Father. Let us represent to ourselves the Father full of delights, rejoicing in the views of this sacrificed body, drawing a perpetual stream of pleasure and sweet smells from the fumes of this sacrifice rising up continually before him. May not this calm our fears, since it smooths the frowns of divine justice? Did the people shout when the ark returned, and shall our hearts be full of fears, when our sacrifice is returned to heaven and has found a gracious reception [acceptance] from that justice [which] we had so highly provoked?

A disconsolate carriage [fearful attitude] in a holy believer implies that God had rejected it [the Cross] as mean and weak, rather than received it as perfect and glorious. A heavy walking [sad mood] is a disparagement [an undervaluing] to the greatness of the sacrifice, and the wisdom and judgment of God the accepter of it. If we should eat our bread with a merry heart, because God hath accepted our works

(Eccles. 9:7), much more since God hath accepted our victim, by whose merits our duties and works smell sweet, that before smelt rank [nasty] by nature. We should therefore draw as much sweetness from this sacrifice for our souls, according to our measures, as God did from it for his own content and satisfaction. It appeased God's fury against us, and should banish our jealousies of God.

(a) If once acceptable to God, then it is for ever acceptable. If once sweet, it is always sweet. God cannot be deceived in his estimations, nor change his value of it, nor can the sacrifice ever become noisome [hateful]. The strength of the divine nature that rendered it at first pleasing preserves its savour for ever. He died to offer it and lives to preserve the virtue of it (Rom. 5:10). The fragrancy conferred upon it by the Deity in conjunction with the humanity is as durable as the Deity itself: he 'sat down on the right hand of God' (Heb. 10:12), after he had offered himself a sacrifice, to exercise the office of a Priest. God would have the Priest and sacrifice for ever in his sight. His priesthood is for ever, his sacrifice therefore is for ever sweet. Without a sacrifice he could not be a Priest. As his priesthood hath a perpetual vigour, so his sacrifice hath a perpetual freshness, and inexhaustible virtue. For the exercise of his office depends upon the continuance of the offering.

The blood of this sacrifice is not compared to a pond, or water in a vessel, though of the largest capacity, but to a living and ever-running fountain, 'a fountain opened to the house of David' (Zech. 13:1). Repentance was hid from the eyes of Christ in offering it for a ransom from the power of the grave, and a redemption from death (Hosea 13:14), and no less is repentance hid from the eyes of God in accepting it. The covenant sealed by it is everlasting, and derives its duration from this blood of the victim (Heb. 13:20); the virtue of it endures as long as the covenant, since if that failed, the covenant would expire, the superstructure not being able to stand if the foundation be rotten.

And from hence an everlasting righteousness is derived, that our persons, odious by Adam, may be beautiful by Christ. At the same time that he made reconciliation for iniquity, he brought in everlasting righteousness (Dan. 9:24), at the same time therefore that God accepted that reconciliation, he accepted that everlasting righteousness for security and justification. He has not pacified God for a few days or years, but for ever (Heb. 10:14). If it were so sweet in the expectation, as to be the ground of the justification of those that hoped for it, it is much more sweet since the oblation and of a stronger efficacy. He is the Captain of the salvation of all the sons that are brought to glory, and that believe. He himself was made 'perfect through sufferings' (Heb. 2:10). The 'twenty-four elders' confessed themselves 'redeemed by this blood' (Rev. 10:8, 9). These are the patriarchs that died before him, as well as the apostles who expired after him.

He was a lamb, a sacrifice 'slain from the foundation of the world' (Rev. 13:8). Not in regard of decree (that were [would be] an unsatisfactory sense of the place [i.e. this text], as it would be to say, a man were dead from the foundation of the world, because it was appointed for him once to die), but in regard of efficacy, and a mystical sprinkling of his blood upon those that lived at the beginning, as well as those that shall live at the end of the world. If it had a savour with God for those that lived before him, it has much more a savour for those that have lived since his actual offering and acceptance.

(b) From this arises pardon of sin. He was a sweet savour as he offered himself, and in the ends [intentions] for which he offered himself. He was a sacrifice for sin. For so those words in Romans 8:3, which we translate 'and for sin' must be understood, and read thus: 'And by a sacrifice for sin, condemned sin in the flesh'. If offered for sin, and accepted as an offering for sin, the consequence of this must be remission. Through the blood of that Beloved, whom he accepted, we have 'redemption through his blood, the forgiveness of sins' (Eph. 1:6, 7), not of one, or two, or a few sins, but all. He was made sin indefinitely, all kind of sin in the extent, as much made sin as he was made accused. As he bore all the curse, so he satisfied for all sin, the greatest as well as the least. So that the blood of this sacrifice 'cleanseth us from all sin' (1 John 1:7) where gospel dispositions are found, from all that from which the law of Moses could not justify: 'And by him all that believe are justified from all things, from which ye could not be justified by the law of Moses' (Acts 13:39).

What was impossible to be done by the sacrifices of the law is completely done by the offering of the Redeemer. The strength of the one is directly opposite to the weakness of the other. It [the law of Mosaic rituals] could not really justify from any, and this is able to justify from all. As it was not over-valued by God, so it cannot be over-balanced by sin; since the judgment of God has passed upon it with an approbation, the monstrousness of guilt is not too great for an expiation. Whatsoever our sins are, yet they have their limits; but God's infinite pleasure in the sacrifice speaks [commends] the merit of it [as] infinite, and the efficacy of it eternal. All sins were at once laid upon the head of this offering (Isa. 53:7). He suffered but once, and therefore at that one time all sins by one act were laid upon his shoulders, 'who his own self bare our sins' (1 Pet. 2:24) and God accepted him 'his own self', and accepted him as he bore them, and glorified him because he purged them (Heb. 1:3). So that though he did but once offer himself, and that for all sins in the bulk, he was received with a welcome, as if he had offered in particular for every sin. And therefore there is no more need of an offering, but a recourse to that one price. To think it is not able to expiate all sin is to undervalue the judgment [which] God has given of his Son, to charge him with a mistake, and to imagine that there is more in sin to ruin than in this sacrifice to repair.

(c) Hence then there can be no condemnation to them that are in Christ. The apostle lays down this conclusion, and confirms it by the reason of his being a sacrifice (Rom. 8:1, 3). They who are presented by Christ, quickened by the virtue of this sacrifice, cannot fall under the stroke of divine justice. If it was offered for those that should believe, it was accepted for such as should believe, it being accepted for the same persons and the same ends for which it was offered, and therefore those persons fundamentally accepted in the acceptance of it and the ends for which it was offered, granted, and concluded on in the act of acceptance. The apostle upon this score breathes out a challenge to all to bring a condemning charge against him. The justice of God, the curse of the law, the charges of conscience and the accusations of devils may be all answered by this: 'It is Christ that died ... It is God that justifieth' (Rom. 8:33, 34). It is Christ that is offered, and God that accepts. Justice cannot condemn; for though his sacrifice was sweet and pleasant to all the perfections of the divine nature, yet justice was the peculiar object of it. God as a Judge delivered him; God as a Judge accepted him. Justice required it, and justice is disarmed by it; justice only was to be contented; mercy required no blood; wisdom stepped in to decide the controversy and make an agreement. If the condemning attribute be satisfied, there is no condemnation to be expected. If it be sweet to justice, justice cannot retain its former frowns; justice cannot be pleased with that, and displeased with those for whom it was offered and accepted, and by whom it is received. It is part of our happiness that we come not only to God as gracious, but [to] God as a Judge: 'To God the Judge of all' (Heb. 12:23).

As Christ was made sin for us, so are we made righteous by him. He was made sin to undergo a condemnation that we might be made righteous and be above a condemnation. It is more efficacious to divert the sword of divine justice from the believing offender than the blood of the paschal lamb was to turn the edge of the angel's sword from the house of an Israelite. The blood of Christ sprinkled cannot be of less force than the blood of a silly [i.e. senseless] lamb, since the efficacy of it was not as it was the blood of a lamb, but the blood of a type, deriving its virtue, not from the subject whence the blood was drawn, but from the person signified, and the sacrifice prefigured, by it. Well then, his condemnation has procured our absolution, and God's acceptance of him hath ensured our liberty. The sweet savour of the sacrifice has overcome the stench of our sins. Though God forsook him for a time, he has now accepted him that he may not abandon us for ever. Neither the wrath of God, nor the malediction of the law is to be feared. God, by this one act, has stopped the course of his vengeance and laid aside the thunders of

Sinai. The flames we had deserved are quenched by the blood flowing from the wounds of this victim; the smoke of our sacrifice shadows us and, in God's acceptance of him, every believer finds his infallible absolution.

(d) Here is a sufficient ground for peace of conscience. Only this can give a repose to our spirits, turn our fears into hopes and our sorrows into songs. If it were a sweet savour to God, whose infinite knowledge was acquainted with the least mite, as well as the greatest mountain in the number of our sins, and whose holiness found an infinite loathsomeness in our iniquities; if it thus contented God, it may settle the agitations of our spirits; and because it stilled fury in God, it may silence troubles in us. If it gave God a delight, who in the knowledge of our sins, loathing of them and condemning for them, is 'greater than our heart[s]' (1 John 3:20), it is a ground of peace to us, who come infinitely short of God in knowing our charge, infinitely short of his holiness in loathing our guilt, and infinitely short of his justice in condemning ourselves. That which has been a sweet savour to pacify God wants not a savour to appease our consciences. Our great inquiry in troubles of spirit is, How shall we appear before God? The answer from this doctrine is, In the smoke of this sacrifice. The impurities of our natures, the sin of our souls and the mixture in our services are purified by this. The sweetness of this sacrifice has sweetened the terrors of the Lord, and rendered man a welcome supplicant to that God before whom he durst [dare] not formerly appear.

(e) Here is a full ground of expectation of all necessary blessings. God accepted it as it was offered; it was offered, not only as a propitiating, but a purchasing sacrifice, and the acceptance of it was in the same quality wherein it was offered (Acts 20:28). His blood was a purchasing blood; he purchased a people for heaven, and purchased heaven for his people. He did not only silence justice with its wrath, but merited heaven with its riches, and shed his blood as a price for the pleasures of paradise. God judged this sacrifice, not only enough to free man from misery, but instate him in happiness; not only to deliver our souls from the pit, but to enlighten us with the light of the living. It was valued by him as a full compensation for the wrongs he had sustained, and a full merit for the blessings we wanted [lacked].

When he found this ransom, his voice was not only 'Deliver him from going down to the pit', but I will make 'His flesh ... fresher than a child's'; a strength and vigour of grace shall be restored in him, as the radical moisture in a child: 'he shall return to the days of his youth: He shall pray unto God, and he will be favourable unto him: and he shall see his face with joy' (Job 33:24-26). The Israelites addressed themselves to the propitiatory (the mercy-seat) not only for the pardon of their sins, but the conferring of other blessings. This is the blood of the covenant, and therefore procures for us the blessings of the covenant. The blessings we want [lack] are often in the gospel ascribed to the merit of this sacrifice, and not simply to the grace of God. The grace of God appointed the sacrifice, but the blessings we receive were merited by it. Our victim was so pleasing to God, and the obedience in it so full of an infinite love to him, that he gained by it the affections of God and a grant of whatsoever was most precious to be bestowed upon those for whom he offered himself, that thereby the pleasure he [i.e. God] took in it might be fully evidenced.

5. *Let us lay hold of it, and plead this sacrifice.*

(a) Let natural men imitate God in an acceptance of this sacrifice. No man perishes for want of God's pleasure in it, but for want of his own acceptance of it upon the gospel conditions. No bitten Israelite perished for want of a brazen serpent, but for want of a look to it. Cast not an aspersion upon God by undervaluing that which he does so highly prize. Be guided by his infallible judgment, rather than by the errors of your own. Think not of it coldly, as if you were indifferent whether you had a share in it or not, since God received it not with an indifferent, but an inconceivable affection. Let that which is sweet to God, be so to us. That which is savoury [pleasing] to that infinite Spirit cannot justly be unsavoury [displeasing] to our contracted souls.

God found no sweetness in the blood of goats or smoke of incense (Ps. 50), but only in this sacrifice; nor should any of us rest in the transitory pleasures of this life, and sing a requiem to our souls from perishing enjoyments, but from the blood of the Lamb that endures for ever. There is no likelihood for a creature to find rest in that wherein God finds none. We are not sure of our lives, but we are sure we are guilty. And shall any of us be unconcerned about a powerful sacrifice?

Let a self-abhorrence possess our souls, without which we can have no esteem of this offering. As God's loathing of sin made him [Christ's sacrifice] value for expiation, so our sense of sin will make us value this for our atonement. Let no man think that unworthy of him, which God thinks not unworthy of himself. He commanded the angels to adore him for it, either when he brought him into the world to be a sacrifice, or brought him into the world above, after he had by his blood 'purged our sins' (Heb. 1:3). God would have men and angels concur [agree] with him in the magnificent acceptance of our Saviour.

(b) Let those that believe continually apply and plead it. This is so sweet to God, that there is no need of a new sacrifice, but there is need of a daily application. There was no need of a new serpent to be erected upon every sting, but there was need of a new looking up to the serpent upon every wound. We can be no more without this [for] one day to comfort our souls than we can be without bread to nourish our bodies. The remembrance of it must come up with the remembrance of every sin in our consciences. In this only shall we find mercy for our iniquities and comfort for our sorrows. What was sweet to God in the acceptance, will be sweet to him in the pleas of it. It has not lost its savour, nor has God changed his judgment. Christ is in the fragrance of his sacrifice with God, as well as in his divinity, the 'same yesterday, today, and for ever'.

We contract a daily guilt and we stand in need of a daily application to this. God will not make us perfect in this life so as to keep up the continual credit of this sacrifice, that we may live by faith, and have every day sensible [conscious] thoughts of the power of this oblation. Let all our pleas with God be founded in his acceptance of this. It is always to be pleaded by us, as it is always eyed by the Father. No pardon is granted but upon the account of it. In every pardoning act, God looks first with pleasure upon this victim, and dips his pen in the blood of it, to blot out the iniquity. No blessing is poured upon us, on which the merit of this sacrifice is not stamped; and no petition [prayer] must be presented by us, but in the virtue of it.

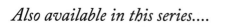
Also available in this series....

The
Pleasantness
of a
Religious Life

Life as good as it can be

MATTHEW HENRY

INTRODUCTION BY J. I. PACKER

978-1-84550-651-3

The Pleasantness of a Religious Life

A Puritan's View of the good life

MATTHEW HENRY

'Here is a bait that has no hook under it…a pleasure which God himself invites you to, and which will make you happy, truly and eternally happy…it is certain that there is true pleasure in true religion.'

Matthew Henry

Matthew Henry, the great Puritan commentator, here looks at what gives people real joy. He looks at twelve different types of Christian pleasure, reviews what God has done to bring sinners joy, demonstrates that Christian experience proves this and challenges the reader to join in!

This was Matthew Henry's last book and was at the press when he died in 1714.

This classic of Christian living is brought to you by J. I. Packer who adds an extensive introduction to the book showing its significance and gestation from Henry's ministry.

'We too get told that being a Christian is a bleak and burdensome business, and not being a Christian could be more fun; we too, like Henry's first hearers and readers, need to be reminded that it is absolutely not so.'

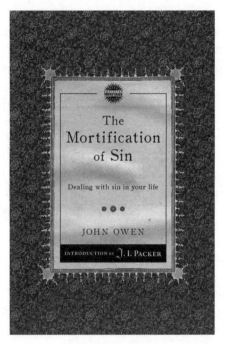

The
Mortification
of Sin

Dealing with sin in your life

JOHN OWEN

INTRODUCTION BY J. I. PACKER

978-1-84550-977-4

The Mortification of Sin

A Puritan's View of how to deal with sin in your life

JOHN OWEN

'I owe more to John Owen than to any other theologian, ancient or modern, and I owe more to this little book than to anything else he wrote.'

J.I Packer

John Owen insisted on the importance of the Christian dealing effectively with their sinful tendencies and attitudes. He believed that God, through his Word and Spirit, had provided the guidelines and the power for this to be achieved.

In this book, John Owen effectively dismisses various excuses for not engaging in self-scrutiny and yet avoids the current trend of self-absorption. In so doing he provides principles to help believers live lives of holiness. 'We too get told that being a Christian is a bleak and burdensome business, and not being a Christian could be more fun; we too, like Henry's first hearers and readers, need to be reminded that it is absolutely not so.'

John Owen (1616-1683) is amongst the best known of the Puritans. His writings continue to be widely read and greatly appreciated to this day.

These Puritan works are now available in the Christian Heritage imprint.

978-1-78191-108-2

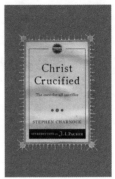

978-1-84550-976-7

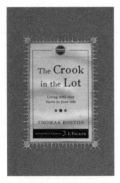

978-1-84550-649-0

978-1-84550-650-6

978-1-84550-648-3

978-1-78191-107-5

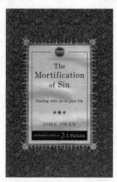

978-1-84550-977-4

978-1-84550-651-3

978-1-84550-975-0

"a treat for anyone with healthy spiritual taste buds."
SINCLAIR B. FERGUSON

PURITAN
PORTRAITS

● ◆ ●

J. I. PACKER
ON SELECTED CLASSIC PASTORS
AND PASTORAL CLASSICS

978-1-84550-700-8

Puritan Portraits

J. I. Packer on Selected Classic Pastors and Pastoral Classics

J. I PACKER

With characteristic ease of style, clarity of thought, and theological insight, Dr Packer introduces us to the life and thought of seven of the all-time masters of what one of them called 'the life of God in the soul of man.' Puritan Portraits is a treat for anyone with healthy spiritual taste buds.

Sinclair B. Ferguson,
Senior Minister, The First Presbyterian Church, Columbia, South Carolina

In an age of trendy fluff, here is solid food for the church and for the soul.

Carl R. Trueman,
Paul Woolley Professor of Historical Theology and Church History, Westminster Theological Seminary, Philadelphia, Pennsylvania.

...simply no better tour guide for exploring Puritan faith and spirituality than J. I. Packer. Highly recommended!

Sam Storms,
Pastor, Bridgeway Church, Oklahoma City, Oklahoma

J. I. Packer can't wait to introduce us to the Puritans' rich theology and deep spirituality. J. I. Packer gives us profiles of John Flavel, Thomas Boston, John Bunyan, Matthew Henry, Henry Scougal, John Owen and Stephen Charnock and two closer portraits of William Perkins and Richard Baxter. J I Packer considers this head-line hitting holiness movement, their analytical thoroughness and literary legacy and the Puritan ideal for pastors. Come and join J. I. Packer as he introduces us to Puritan literature which he helps to bring alive for today's audience.

J. I. Packer is named by *Time* Magazine as one of the 25 most influential evangelicals alive. He is the Board of Governor's Professor of Theology at Regent College, Vancouver, BC, Canada.

Christian Focus Publications
publishes books for all ages

Our mission statement –

STAYING FAITHFUL
In dependence upon God we seek to impact the world through literature faithful to His infallible Word, the Bible. Our aim is to ensure that the LORD Jesus Christ is presented as the only hope to obtain forgiveness of sin, live a useful life and look forward to heaven with Him.

REACHING OUT
Christ's last command requires us to reach out to our world with His gospel. We seek to help fulfil that by publishing books that point people towards Jesus and help them develop a Christ-like maturity. We aim to equip all levels of readers for life, work, ministry and mission.

Books in our adult range are published in three imprints.

Christian Focus contains popular works including biographies, commentaries, basic doctrine and Christian living. Our children's books are also published in this imprint.

Mentor focuses on books written at a level suitable for Bible College and seminary students, pastors, and other serious readers. The imprint includes commentaries, doctrinal studies, examination of current issues and church history.

Christian Heritage contains classic writings from the past.

Christian Focus Publications Ltd,
Geanies House, Fearn, Ross-shire,
IV20 1TW, Scotland, United Kingdom
info@christianfocus.com
www.christianfocus.com